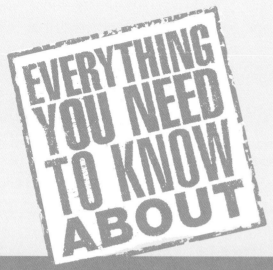

EVERYTHING YOU NEED TO KNOW ABOUT

WORLD HISTORY
HOMEWORK

ANNE ZEMAN

KATE KELLY

AN IRVING PLACE PRESS BOOK

SCHOLASTIC INC.
NEW YORK TORONTO LONDON AUCKLAND
SYDNEY MEXICO CITY NEW DELHI HONG KONG

ISBN 978-0-545-37476-7

12 11 10 9 8 7 6 5 4 3 2 1   11 12 13 14 15 16/0

Printed in the U.S.A.   08

This edition first printing, September 2011

Cover design, Red Herring Design; Cover illustration, Sarajo Frieden
Interior design, Bennett Gewirtz, Gewirtz Graphics, Inc.; Interior illustration, Greg Paprocki

Grateful acknowledgment is made to:
FPG International, for permission to reprint photographs on pages 37, 67, and 94.
The Library of Congress, for permission to reprint photographs on pages 95, 98, 100, and 101.
The Scholastic Picture Research Department, for permission to reprint photographs
on pages 31, 35, 47, 52, 54, 67, 70, 90, 94, 99, and 101 (photo, Hideki Tojo).

Contents

Part 7. The Modern World (1700–Present)

Appendix: The World in Focus

Index

Introduction

It's time to do your homework—but you have questions. You need some help, but no adults are around, and you can't reach your classmates on the phone. Where can you go for help?

What Questions Does This Book Answer?

In *Everything You Need to Know About World History Homework*, you will find a wealth of information, including answers to some of the most commonly asked world history homework questions, like

- Where is the Fertile Crescent, and what happened there? The Fertile Crescent and the civilization it supported are described on pages 2–5.

- When were the great pyramids of Egypt built, and what was their purpose? Find out about the great pyramids on pages 11–12.

- What was Hammurabi's Code, and on what principles was it based? Hammurabi's Code is explained on page 4.

- Where and when were the first Olympic Games? The Olympic Games are the subject of a feature on page 17.

- What is democracy? A direct democracy? An indirect democracy? The principle of democracy is clarified on page 16.

- Where were the first civilizations in India? A history of early India is found on pages 26–30.

- Which of the world's three major religions developed in the Middle East? The major world religions that sprang from the Middle East are described on pages 38–42.

- What is the gold-salt trade? Where did it take place? The gold-salt trade is described on page 44.

- What was feudalism like in Europe and Japan? Feudalism is explained on pages 36, 73, and 86.

- What is capitalism? What is communism? Capitalism and communism are compared on page 90.

- What is the International Space Station, and who created it? The ISS and milestones in space exploration are discussed on page 114.

What Is the *Everything You Need to Know About…Homework* series?

The *Everything You Need to Know About…Homework* series is a set of unique reference resources written especially to answer the homework questions of fourth, fifth, and sixth graders. The series provides information to answer commonly asked homework questions in a variety of subjects. Here you'll find facts, charts, definitions, and explanations, complete with examples and illustrations that will supplement schoolwork colorfully, clearly, and comprehensively.

A Note to Parents

It's important to support your children's efforts to do homework. Welcome their questions and see that they have access to a well-lighted desk or table, pencils, paper, and any other books or equipment that they need—such as rulers, calculators, reference books or textbooks, and so on. You might also set aside a special time each day for doing homework, a time when you're available to answer questions that may arise. But don't do you child's homework for them. Remember, homework should create a bond between school and home. It is meant to enhance the lessons taught at school on a daily basis, and to promote good work and study habits. Although it is gratifying to have your children present flawless homework papers, the flawlessness should be a result of your children's explorations and efforts—not your own.

The *Everything You Need to Know About…Homework* series is designed to help your children complete their homework on their own to the best of their abilities. If they're stuck, you can use these books with them to help find answers to troubling homework problems. And remember, when the work is finished, praise your children for a job well done.

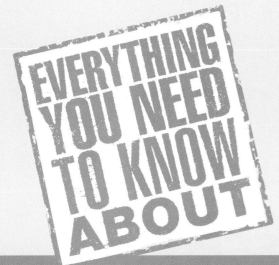

EVERYTHING YOU NEED TO KNOW ABOUT

WORLD HISTORY HOMEWORK

Chapter 1 # The Fertile Crescent

Civilization began in the area known as the Fertile Crescent. (A civilization is a human organization that involves a central government, permanent buildings, food production, and, sometimes, a system of writing.) The Fertile Crescent was a piece of land that stretched from the eastern shore of the Mediterranean Sea to the Persian Gulf. It got its name because the soil was rich and it was shaped like a crescent.

The eastern section of the Fertile Crescent, between the Tigris and Euphrates rivers, was called **Mesopotamia**. Mesopotamia means "land between the rivers." The western part of the Fertile Crescent was called the **Phoenicia** section.

The civilization of Sumer begins	The powerful kingdom of Egypt begins	The Egyptians build the great pyramids and monuments	The city of Babylon is settled along the Euphrates River	The Hittite empire is among the first to use iron	The Assyrians build a powerful empire	Moses leads the Hebrews out of Egypt and back to Canaan, their homeland	The Phoenicians invent an alphabet	Persia conquers Asia Minor and the Fertile Crescent
It develops the first written language								
3500 B.C.	**3000**	**2700–2100**	**2000**	**1750**	**1350**	**1250**	**1200**	**550**

The Sumerians

In the southern part of Mesopotamia was an area known as Sumer. The Sumerians were one of the first people known to live in the Fertile Crescent. They lived there from about 3500 to 2000 B.C.

The Sumerians farmed and raised cattle. Many were tradespeople and artisans (craftspeople) who lived in cities. In the cities, the Sumerians built huge temples and monuments. They invented the arch and the **ziggurat**, a temple shaped like a pyramid with terraces and steps. One of their cities was called Ur. This city was found buried in sand in 1927, along with many graves and artifacts. The graves that were found turned out to be the tombs of kings. The people who unearthed these tombs, called **archaeologists**, discovered a number of things about the Sumerians:

• **They were skilled builders and artists.**

• **They had an alphabet and knew how to write.**

• **Their army was supplied with weapons.**

• **Their metals, stones, and wood were obtained from trading with other peoples.**

• **Kings were treated as gods who had great power and wealth.**

Sumer consisted of three classes of people. The upper class included kings, nobles, priests, wealthy landowners, and government officials. The middle class was made up of merchants, farmers, tradespeople, and soldiers. The lowest class was made up of slaves.

ACCOMPLISHMENTS OF THE SUMERIANS

1 They developed the first written language, a system of writing called cuneiform. The alphabet consisted of about 500 characters, or wedge-shaped forms.

2 They studied science and mathematics. Their skills in mathematics were so developed that they created a system for subdividing a day and a year as well as dividing a circle into 360 parts.

3 They were skillful in using the wheel and made vehicles for farming, moving goods for trade, and fighting enemies.

The Golden Age of Athens

Julius Caesar takes power in Rome

500–430   **49 B.C.**

The Babylonians

The city of Babylon was located on the Euphrates River. It was founded about 2000 B.C. and is part of present-day Iraq. Babylon became the capital of the empire of Babylonia and was an important center for trade and religious worship. The city included splendid temples to the **deities** (the gods and goddesses they worshiped).

One of the greatest kings of Babylon was **Hammurabi**, who ruled for forty-two years, from 1792 to 1750 B.C. He recorded a set of laws for his people. Hammurabi's Code of Laws consisted of 282 laws and was probably displayed in every Babylonian town. Hammurabi based his laws on the principle that the strong should not injure the weak. These laws created a reasonable tax system, set fair prices and wages, acknowledged the rights of women (including allowing them to own property), and set up a strong system of punishments for the guilty.

Another famous king was **Nebuchadnezzar II.** He ruled Babylonia for forty-three years, from 605 to 562 B.C., and is mentioned in the Bible. Nebuchadnezzar II conquered Jerusalem and forced thousands of people to move to Babylon to live in captivity. He also captured the cities of Tyre and Judah.

Nebuchadnezzar II spent enormous amounts of money in building up Babylon, and its Hanging Gardens eventually became a wonder of the ancient world (see p. 25). He is said to have gone mad toward the end of his life; Babylon grew weaker when he died.

ACCOMPLISHMENTS OF THE BABYLONIANS

1 They established a code of laws known as Hammurabi's Code.

2 They believed in astrology, which holds that the movements of the stars and planets have a direct effect on human life. Their recognition of the different planets and stars led to the scientific study of astronomy, the study of the universe.

The Assyrians

Starting about 1350 B.C., the Assyrians lived in the area where the Sumerians had once lived. They were traders and fierce warriors who built a mighty empire by conquering others with their highly skilled army. When enemies were captured they were either taken as slaves or murdered. Sometimes the Assyrians destroyed entire cities, such as the city of Elam, conquered in 640 B.C.

The Assyrians conquered the Fertile Crescent, including Babylon and Egypt. Their capital was at Nineveh. The empire grew wealthy from the cities the Assyrians captured and the taxes they collected from the defeated peoples.

The last great king of Assyria was **Ashurbanipal.** His library held a great deal of information about Assyria. It was the first known library and contained more than 22,000 clay tablets written in Sumerian cuneiform. These tablet "books" included proverbs, fables, and folktales, as well as writings on religion, science, law, and magic.

The Assyrian Empire lasted more than 700 years, to 612 B.C., when the Babylonians and the Medes destroyed Nineveh.

ACCOMPLISHMENTS OF THE ASSYRIANS

1 They built a system of roads.

2 They instituted a form of government for the provinces in which a governor was appointed to oversee the king's territory.

3 They established the first library.

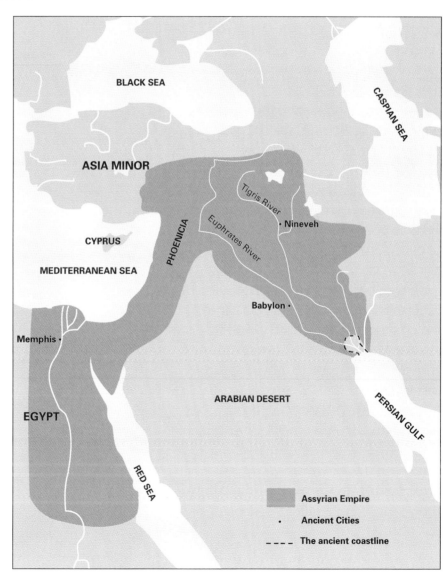

The Assyrian Empire around 650 B.C.

BLACK SEA

CASPIAN SEA

ASIA MINOR

Tigris River

Euphrates River

• Nineveh

CYPRUS

PHOENICIA

MEDITERRANEAN SEA

Babylon •

Memphis •

ARABIAN DESERT

PERSIAN GULF

EGYPT

RED SEA

Assyrian Empire

• Ancient Cities

- - - - The ancient coastline

The Hebrews

The Hebrews, the ancestors of today's Jews, were nomads, or wanderers, in the Ancient Middle East, probably beginning at about 1800 B.C. We know their story almost entirely from the first part of the Bible, known as the Old Testament.

The Old Testament tells the story of a family of nomads from Canaan, a narrow strip of land between the Mediterranean Sea and the Jordan River, who were forced to go to Egypt by a severe drought in their native land. Like many other foreign peoples, they were made slaves in Egypt. Their descendants escaped at about 1250 B.C., led by **Moses**. This escape from Egypt came to be known as the **Exodus**, which means "going out."

After leaving Egypt, the Hebrews defeated many other peoples of Canaan and eventually settled in Palestine, making a capital at Jerusalem in about 1000 B.C. There they prospered under three great kings—**Saul**, **David**, and **Solomon**. The kingdom split into two after Solomon's death—Israel in the north and Judah in the south.

During all this time, the Hebrews were developing a set of religious beliefs that were to become modern Judaism, and strongly influence Christianity and Islam as well.

The Hebrews believed that there was only one God—an idea called **monotheism**. The other religions of the Fertile Crescent had many gods. Each god had his or her job. One watched over the crops; one helped women have children; another supported his people in war. Other religions usually also had a creation god, one who people believed had created the world, and personal gods, from whom a person could ask small favors.

The Hebrews believed that one God was responsible for all of these things. The same God who created the world also helped his people in war, helped them to have children, made the rain, and listened to the prayers of every person.

The Hebrews believed that God shouldn't be represented by a statue, so they didn't have statues of God the way their neighbors did.

They also had a set of laws, including the **Ten Commandments**, that told them how to live their lives.

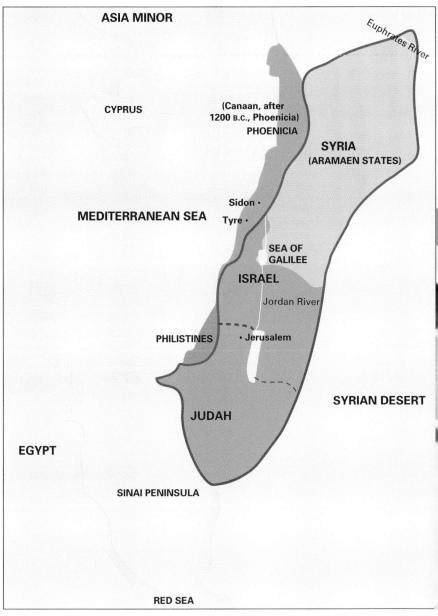

The Hebrews and Phoenicians shared a narrow strip of land along the eastern coast of the Mediterranean Sea.

ACCOMPLISHMENTS OF THE HEBREWS

1 They believed in a single all-powerful God.

2 They were the first to record the Old Testament of the Bible.

3 Their high moral behavior, founded on the Ten Commandments, set new standards.

4 Their prophets fought for justice for the poor and weak.

The Phoenicians

The Phoenicians lived in small city-states along the Mediterranean coast, in present-day Lebanon, from about 1200 to 800 B.C. Tyre and Sidon were their chief cities. The Phoenicians were the most famous traders of the ancient world. They turned to trade because they had little land to farm. They were skilled shipbuilders and master sailors, becoming one of the first people to sail at night by the stars. The Phoenicians were also explorers. They sailed across the Mediterranean and built colonies such as Carthage in North Africa.

Many Phoenicians became wealthy. They controlled trade throughout the Mediterranean area for nearly 300 years. They traded their wool, papyrus, ivory, and glass for goods they needed. One of the products the Phoenicians were most known for was a vivid purple dye made from tiny shells. It was so expensive to make that only very wealthy people could buy purple cloth. It became the favorite color of royalty.

ACCOMPLISHMENTS OF THE PHOENICIANS

1 They invented an alphabet. In order to keep business records of their trade, the Phoenicians developed a system of writing. The Phoenician alphabet contained 22 letters and, unlike cuneiform and hieroglyphics, the letters represented the sounds of the human voice. This made it much easier to read and write. Because the Phoenicians traveled so much, they spread the use of the alphabet to many places.

2 They developed artistic skills, such as carving ivory figures and making colored glass ornaments.

3 They traded all over the Mediterranean, spreading both their own goods and those of their trading partners.

The Persians

The Persians lived east of the Fertile Crescent on the plateau of present-day Iran. They were warriors on horseback who came from central Asia. Their capital city was Persepolis. It was built by the **Achaemenid** family, who ruled the Persian Empire from 550 to 330 B.C. As rulers, the Persians were generous to the people they conquered.

Cyrus the Great ruled from 559 to 530 B.C. and expanded the Persian Empire by conquering Asia Minor and eventually the Fertile Crescent. Under **King Darius I**, the empire was extended eastward as far as the Indus River in India. It was during his reign that the building of Persepolis began. He was often called **Darius the Great** because he restored order and made many improvements to the empire. Because the empire was so large, Darius divided it into twenty provinces, each ruled by an official called a **satrap**. The government built roads to improve trade and the movement of the army.

Persia fought several wars with the Greek city-states (see p. 15). In 330 B.C., Persia fell to the army of **Alexander the Great** (see p. 19).

ACCOMPLISHMENTS OF THE PERSIANS

1 They divided their empire into provinces for easier rule.

2 They built roads and canals.

3 They wrote the Avesta, a religious book based on the beliefs of the prophet Zoroaster.

Zoroastrian priests carried a staff with a bull's head as a symbol of their religious battle against evil.

The Hittites

The Hittites lived in the mountains near modern Turkey. Their empire was established by 1750 B.C. and was known as **Hatti**. Its capital was **Hattusa**. Hattusa was 3,000 feet above sea level and surrounded by mountains as well as a stone wall up to twenty-six feet thick. The Hittites built a powerful empire that lasted about 550 years.

The Hittite rulers were the first to use a treaty to settle differences with other peoples. **King Hattusili III** and **King Ramses II** of Egypt signed a treaty in 1284 B.C. They agreed not to make war on each other, to help each other if attacked by a third party, and to respect each other's borders. It was one of the first treaties signed by two great empires.

ACCOMPLISHMENTS OF THE HITTITES

1 They were among the first people to use iron. Before this, people used copper and bronze to make tools and weapons, but these soft metals bent and broke easily. Since iron is harder, it makes better weapons. This was one of the most important accomplishments of the ancient world.

2 They signed some of the first treaties.

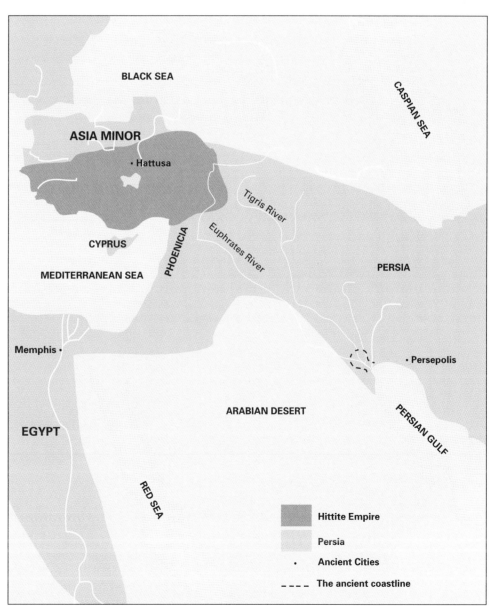

The Hittite Empire covered much of Asia Minor in present-day Turkey. The Persian Empire stretched from the borders of India to the Nile River in Egypt. Persepolis was the capital of Persia.

The First Civilization of Ancient Egypt

Ancient Egypt was one of the earliest civilizations. It was located in northeast Africa and began about 5,000 years ago along the Nile River. Ancient Egyptian civilization lasted for about 3,000 years, from 3100 to 332 B.C.

Ancient Egypt was called the gift of the Nile (see p. 11). Egyptians depended on the river for food and work. The people worked together to build irrigation systems to bring water from the Nile to other fields for their crops.

The Egyptians were the first people to make paper, and theirs was the first civilization with a written history. Paper was made from papyrus reed. Ropes, mats, and even boats were also made from papyrus reed. Egyptians were also excellent engineers and builders. They built the great pyramids, temples, statues, and many other buildings. They forced thousands of slaves to work on these buildings.

The Egyptian language was based on **hieroglyphics**. The Egyptians wrote laws, books, prayers, and hymns. They also did mathematics and invented a calendar.

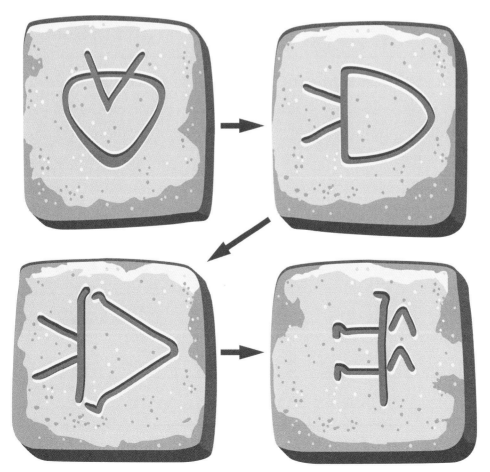

The Egyptians developed hieroglyphics, or picture writing, as seen in this description of an ox.

The Nile River

The Nile River was the center of life for the Egyptians. It is the longest river in the world. It starts in central Africa and flows 4,000 miles north to the Mediterranean Sea. Ancient Egyptian civilization began in the **Nile Delta**, where the river enters the Mediterranean Sea and forms a marshy plain of river mud.

Every year the Nile River flooded and left a rich layer of soil that was good for growing crops. This rich soil was very important to the Egyptians since there is a desert on both sides of the Nile, where little rainfall occurs.

The Nile Delta

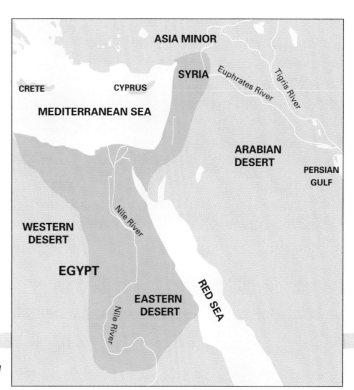

Daily Life of Egyptians

Farming was the chief work in Egypt, and people learned to work the ground to produce wheat, barley, and vegetables. They used donkeys for heavy labor. The men also hunted wild animals and fished. Families lived in houses made of mud, brick, and wood. They often kept small farm animals, like goats or geese. Some raised cattle and sheep for food. Women wove linen and wool for clothing and cooked the meals. Bread and beer were main items in every home. Children helped in the farming and with the household chores.

Some people made crafts such as jewelry, tapestries, pottery, dishes, and metal objects. Others were scribes, the only people who knew how to write. They wrote with pens made from reeds on paper made from papyrus. Scribes usually worked for officials.

The king was regarded as a god and was very powerful. In Egypt the king was called the **pharaoh**. He (and, at least once, she) was considered the earthly leader of the gods. Egyptians worshiped many gods and built temples of brick and stone for them. The great pyramids were built as tombs for the pharaohs. When they died, the pharaohs and their treasures were put in the pyramids.

Builder's escape shaft

Passageway

Underground room

Entrance

11

The Kingdoms of Egypt

Before 3000 B.C., Egypt was divided into the kingdoms of Lower Egypt, in the Nile Delta, and Upper Egypt. **Menes**, a king from the south, conquered and joined the two lands. Menes was the first pharaoh. His dynasty was called the First Dynasty. A **dynasty** is a series of rulers from the same family.

Thirty dynasties ruled Egypt for 3,000 years. Most of the pharaohs were men. Usually, the only women who had important titles were priestesses. However, there was a female pharaoh—**Queen Hatshepsut**. She was the daughter of **King Thutmose I**. He was determined that she follow him, and he instructed the nobles of the royal court that she would be the next ruler. Hatshepsut became queen upon the death of her father, about 1500 B.C. She later took a husband, **Thutmose II.** After his death, she crowned herself King Hatshepsut and became pharaoh. During her reign, Egypt rose to great power and wealth. It was a golden age of peace and prosperity.

Because Egypt's history is so long, historians divide it into three periods—the Old Kingdom, the Middle Kingdom, and the New Kingdom.

PERIOD	DATE	HIGHLIGHTS
Old Kingdom	2700 – 2200 B.C.	The capital was Memphis and then Heliopolis. The great pyramids and the Sphinx, a large statue with a head of a man and body of a lion, were built.
Middle Kingdom	2100 – 1800 B.C.	Egyptian civilization reached great heights. Engineering projects such as irrigation ditches and canals were built. Egypt was conquered by invaders but then recovered. There were several capitals during this era, including Thebes and Memphis.
New Kingdom	1700 – 1100 B.C.	This era is also called the Empire, and the capital was Thebes. Egypt conquered many areas during this time. About 1100 B.C., its great power had begun to decline.

AKHENATEN: The Pharaoh Who Worshiped One God

The pharaoh **Amenhotep IV** wanted the Egyptians to stop worshiping many **deities** (gods and goddesses). He wanted them to worship only one god, the sun god, **Aten**. He closed the great temple of Amon, "the king of gods," at Thebes. Amenhotep wanted to remove all aspects of Amon. To prove he was serious, Amenhotep changed his name to **Akhenaten**, which means "spirit of Aten." He even created a new capital city devoted to Aten. He named the city Akhetaton; it is known today as Tel el Amarna.

Akhenaten, whose reign was roughly from 1352 to 1332 B.C., was one of the first people ever to believe in only one god. His people followed him, but the pharaohs, after his death, restored the old deities.

The Tomb of King Tutankhamen

In 1922 a great discovery was made—the tomb of the pharaoh **Tutankhamen**. Unlike other ancient tombs, this one had not been robbed because it was so well hidden. The magnificent treasures in the tomb gave new insight into ancient Egypt and the skilled work of its artists.

The tomb contained four rooms and each contained the king's personal possessions. There were thrones, beds, chariots, clothes, and statues of gods. Many of the items were made of gold, ivory, and precious stones. The coffin was the most magnificent. It was made of solid gold and contained a headpiece in the likeness of King Tutankhamen made of gold, ebony, and turquoise. This headpiece is considered one of the most beautiful treasures in the world and is on display in Cairo, Egypt.

Successor to Akhenaten, Tutankhamen became king when he was only nine years old. He ruled Egypt for only ten years. During his reign, he restored many temples and recognized the old gods. Very little is known of Tutankhamen's life. He died unexpectedly at eighteen or nineteen years of age, around 1350 B.C.

13

ACCOMPLISHMENTS OF THE EGYPTIANS

1 They made paper from the papyrus reed plant.

2 They invented a calendar.

3 They built the great pyramids.

4 They invented the shadoof, a cranelike device for lifting water from the Nile.

5 They used a loom to weave cloth for clothing.

6 They invented hieroglyphics, a system of writing using characters in the form of pictures.

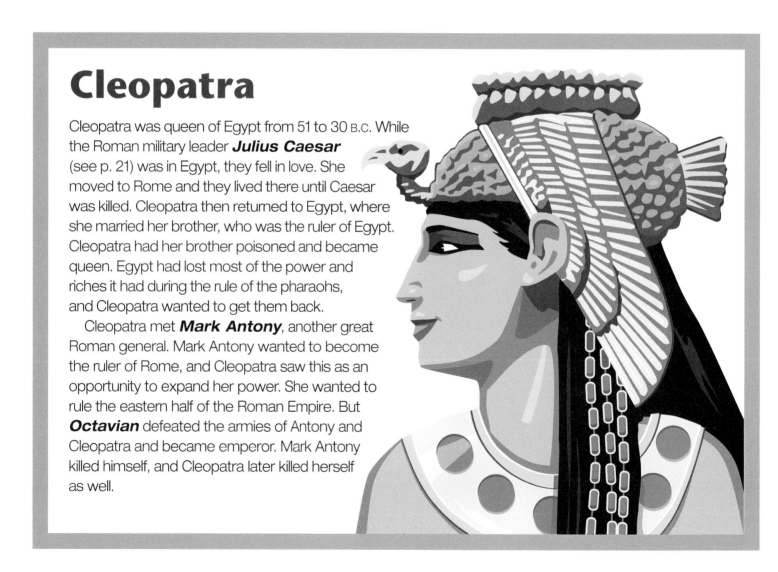

Cleopatra

Cleopatra was queen of Egypt from 51 to 30 B.C. While the Roman military leader *Julius Caesar* (see p. 21) was in Egypt, they fell in love. She moved to Rome and they lived there until Caesar was killed. Cleopatra then returned to Egypt, where she married her brother, who was the ruler of Egypt. Cleopatra had her brother poisoned and became queen. Egypt had lost most of the power and riches it had during the rule of the pharaohs, and Cleopatra wanted to get them back.

Cleopatra met *Mark Antony*, another great Roman general. Mark Antony wanted to become the ruler of Rome, and Cleopatra saw this as an opportunity to expand her power. She wanted to rule the eastern half of the Roman Empire. But *Octavian* defeated the armies of Antony and Cleopatra and became emperor. Mark Antony killed himself, and Cleopatra later killed herself as well.

Ancient Greece

Greeks lived in southeast Europe almost 3,000 years ago. They built Sparta, Athens, and other famous cities. Greece was divided into **city-states.** This meant that each city was like a separate, small nation, with its own laws and government. Even though the city-states operated independently, all of Greece shared the same language and culture. Although Greece had many city-states, the most famous and powerful were Athens and Sparta. They were located on the Peloponnesian Peninsula.

Early Greek City-States of Athens and Sparta

Athens and Sparta were strong in different ways. Athens became a great democracy (a form of government ruled by its people) and was governed by all the free males in the city. Sparta was a military state ruled by a small group of people. Athens became wealthy from its trade and colonies. The wealth of Sparta came from the work of slaves. There was great rivalry between Athens and Sparta, which eventually led to a war for rule of Greece in 431 B.C.

The Parthenon is a temple dedicated to the Greek goddess Athena built at Athens, Greece, in the fifth century B.C.

Athens

Athens became especially prosperous during the period from 500 to 430 B.C. This period is called the **Golden Age of Athens**. It is also known as the **Golden Age of Pericles** because **Pericles**, a famous politician and speaker, was able to influence government voting on various issues. One of his most important achievements was to organize the rebuilding of the Acropolis, a hill where a group of temples had been destroyed by the Persians. This included the Parthenon, one of the most famous buildings of ancient Greece.

The Golden Age of Athens was a time of great writing and learning. During this time, Athens became the center of Greek civilization and culture. Many great artists and thinkers came to Athens and thrived. Great architecture and sculpture was created and plays were performed in open-air theaters.

Philosophy also thrived during this era. Philosophy means "the love of knowledge and wisdom." **Socrates** was a great Athenian philosopher. He was a teacher who asked his students careful questions. In order to answer these questions, the students would be forced to learn how to think. One of his students, Plato, wrote down the talks of Socrates and his pupils. **Plato** also became a teacher and a philosopher, and one of his most famous philosophy students was **Aristotle**. Aristotle was one of the first to look for the truth about things by testing facts and organizing ideas in a logical way. He was a scientist as well as a philosopher.

Sparta

Sparta was a military state. Its soldiers became the most powerful in Greece and were known for their bravery. Every male Spartan had to become a soldier. Young boys left their homes when they were seven years old to begin their military training. They were taught to be loyal to the state and to obey orders. Men had to serve in the army until they were sixty years of age.

Spartan women were treated differently from Athenian women. They were citizens and were viewed as equals to men. Women did not become soldiers, but young girls had to stay physically fit and were trained in gymnastics, boxing, wrestling, and running. Women usually married by the age of twenty and were encouraged to have many children.

The Spartans conquered Messenia and made slaves of the people. The slaves were used to work the land and construct buildings. About 650 B.C., the slaves revolted. It took about twenty years for Sparta to regain total control.

Because of their emphasis on the military, Spartans did little in the arts and sciences. Today, when we use the word **spartan**, we mean plain and uncomplaining. Spartans viewed the Athenian way of life with scorn. In 431 B.C., the Peloponnesian War broke out. Sparta defeated Athens after twenty-seven years of war.

The First Democracy

Athenians believed that the citizens of a country should govern that country. This was the beginning of **democracy**, a form of government in which the people rule.

The Assembly in Athens passed the laws. Every citizen of Athens was a member of the Assembly. This is an example of a **direct democracy**, where citizens participate directly in the government. (The United States has a **representative democracy**, where representatives are chosen to represent groups of people.)

Only free Athenian males could be citizens. A young man could take part in government when he was eighteen years old by attending the Assembly. Women could not take part in government. Neither could males who were from other countries or who were slaves.

The Gods of Olympus

Greek gods were important to the Greek way of life. The Greeks worshiped many gods and goddesses and invented stories, or myths, about them. Each god or goddess was a ruler of some part of nature or human life. Here are some of the gods and goddesses:

Zeus	The king of gods. He was the all-wise ruler of all the gods of the sacred mountain of Olympus (where the gods lived) and protected Greece. He was also the god of the sky and of thunder. The Olympic Games were held in his honor.
Athena	The daughter of Zeus and the patroness of Athens. She was the goddess of wisdom, courage, and victory. The Parthenon was built in her honor.
Apollo	The son of Zeus and twin brother of Artemis. He was the god of sun and light.
Hera	The sister and one of the wives of Zeus. She was the goddess of marriage and women.
Artemis	The twin sister of Apollo. She was the moon goddess and the protector of wild animals. Her arrows brought death.
Hermes	The messenger of the gods and the god of travelers and traders.
Poseidon	The brother of Zeus who ruled all the seas and rivers. It was thought that he caused earthquakes.
Aphrodite	The goddess of love and beauty. She was the most beautiful of the goddesses and she protected lovers.
Ares	The god of war. He was hated by the other gods because of his violence.
Hestia	The goddess of the hearth. She was one of the most loved goddesses because she protected the city, home, and family. Every home had a shrine to her.
Hades	The brother of Zeus and god of the underworld. He ruled the kingdom of the dead.
Demeter	The goddess of agriculture, plants, and the harvest. She caused changes in the seasons.

The Olympics

One of the great religious festivals in Greece was held in the town of Olympia in honor of Zeus. This festival lasted five days and featured competition in sports, music, and drama. It was held every four years. All wars stopped so that people from all over Greece could travel safely to Olympia. At the end of the games, oxen were sacrificed to Zeus, and everyone joined in a great feast.

The main event at the Olympic Games was the **pentathlon.** This competition included five different sports in which an athlete had to compete. It included a foot race, discus throwing, long jump, javelin throwing, and wrestling. The Olympic Games also included running, chariot races, horse races, and boxing matches.

Our modern Olympic Games are copied from this festival. They were started again after many centuries in A.D. 1896 by a Frenchman named **Baron Pierre de Coubertin.**

ACCOMPLISHMENTS OF THE GREEKS

1 They developed the world's first democracy.

2 They were the first people to take a scientific approach to medicine by observing and carefully studying diseases. Hippocrates is known as the father of medicine.

3 Playwrights wrote and produced the first dramas in outdoor theaters. Euripides and Sophocles are two of the most famous playwrights.

4 They invented the rules of geometry as well as other mathematics. Euclid, a mathematician, wrote a geometry text called *Elements*. Only the Bible has been more widely studied.

5 They developed the art of philosophy to search for wisdom and truth. Three of the world's greatest philosophers were Socrates, Plato, and Aristotle.

6 They created outstanding literature and poetry. Two great poems, *The Iliad* and *The Odyssey*, told by Homer, are still read today. Sappho, a female poet, wrote beautiful love poems.

7 They wrote the first histories.

8 They studied and described a way to classify, or group, different types of plants.

9 They created magnificent buildings and beautiful sculpture. Greek architecture made heavy use of columns, which were decorated in different ways.

Greek Columns

Greeks were also brilliant architects. Among their many contributions to building are three styles of columns: Doric, Corinthian, and Ionic.

Doric   *Corinthian*   *Ionic*

Alexander the Great

King ***Philip II of Macedonia*** defeated the weakened city-states of Greece after the Peloponnesian War and became the ruler of all Greece. Philip united all the city-states of Greece and formed one country. He was murdered, but after his death, his son Alexander, who became known as ***Alexander the Great***, took over. He was twenty years old at the time. By the time he was twenty-two, in 334 B.C., he led his army into Persia and defeated King ***Darius*** (see page 8).

Alexander's empire was the largest in the ancient world. It stretched from Greece in the west to India in the east. Alexander spread Greek culture to many areas in his empire. He established great cities throughout, including Alexandria on the Nile in Egypt. Alexander wanted to unite all the peoples of his land, but he did not live to see his plan fulfilled. He died when he was only thirty-two years old.

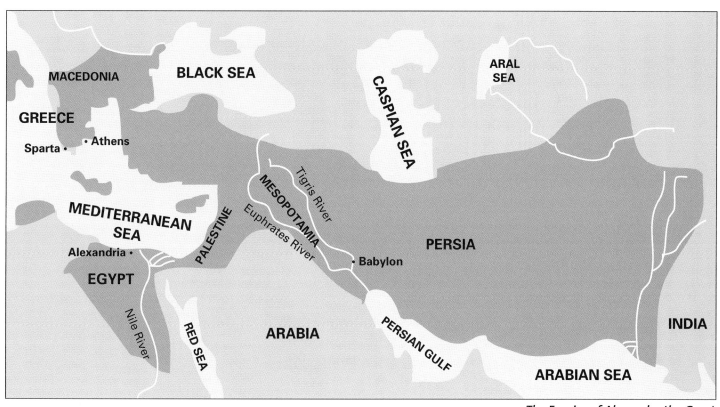

The Empire of Alexander the Great

Chapter 4

Ancient Rome

The city of Rome began as a group of small villages in an area of seven hills on the Tiber River in southern Europe. The villages grew in the hills until they became one large town. This town eventually became the largest empire in the world, with hundreds of nationalities and tribes and almost 100 million people.

The Roman Republic

Around 750 B.C., a people called Etruscans invaded and conquered Rome. They ruled for about 200 years. Romans overthrew their king around 500 B.C. and drove out the Etruscans. The people of Rome set up a new form of government called a **republic**. A republic is a form of government where there is no king and the citizens choose the people to run the government. Free men were allowed to vote, but women and slaves were not.

Roman citizens were divided into two classes: The **patricians** were rich nobles and the **plebeians** were common people, such as farmers and workers. In the early years of the republic, the patricians controlled the government. Only patricians could enter the Senate, where laws were made. The plebeians had little voice in the government and many of the laws were unfair to them.

After more than one hundred years of struggle, the plebeians made a few gains. They won the right to have the laws written down and displayed in the public areas so that the laws could not be suddenly changed. They also gained the right to elect two officers, called **consuls**, to look after interests of the ordinary citizens. The Roman Republic lasted until 27 B.C., when Augustus became emperor.

By the second century B.C., Rome had become a powerful state. Its mighty army conquered all of Italy and eventually ruled all the lands around the Mediterranean Sea. It had even conquered the Greeks. Rome's chief enemy was Carthage in North Africa. Rome and Carthage fought three wars over the course of a hundred years; they were called the **Punic Wars**. They ended when Rome burned Carthage to the ground in 146 B.C.

The lands ruled by the Romans were called **provinces**. Roman provinces had to pay taxes to Rome. The capital became very rich. Rome itself became a city of the very rich and the very poor. Governing such a large empire was difficult, and the Romans began to turn to military leaders as rulers.

The Beginning of the Roman Empire

In 46 B.C., a great general and military hero named **Julius Caesar** took power in Rome. As the dictator, Caesar built new buildings, reduced taxes, and made life better for the plebeians. Julius Caesar was their hero. Because of his military leadership, soldiers were loyal to him. But the Senate, made up of patricians, thought he had too much power. So, in 44 B.C., some senators murdered him.

Caesar's adopted son, **Octavian**, took power in 27 B.C. He called himself **Augustus**, which means "great." Augustus became the first emperor of Rome, which was no longer a republic. This was the beginning of the Roman Empire. Augustus's rule began a 200-year period known as the **Pax Romana**, or the Roman Peace. It was mostly a time of peace and progress.

Augustus ruled from 27 B.C. to A.D. 14. He was a fair and able ruler and did many things for the Roman Empire: He maintained the peace, restored order in the army, established fair taxes, constructed many roads and buildings, and encouraged science, art, and literature.

Rome had a number of strong and able emperors who ruled for many years, expanding the territories and maintaining peace. With the death of **Marcus Aurelius**, in A.D. 180, a long decline began.

Julius Caesar

The Decline and Fall of Rome

The Roman Empire stretched from the Middle East to Great Britain. It was so large that Alexander the Great's empire was just an eastern province. Because of its vastness, it was hard to control. About A.D. 290, the emperor **Diocletian** divided the empire into two sections—the **Western Empire** and the **Eastern Empire**. Diocletian began the shift of power from Rome, the capital of the Western Empire, to the east. Once Emperor **Constantine** took over, in A.D. 324, he completed the shift, making Constantinople the main capital when the city was rebuilt in A.D. 330 (see pp. 38–39).

In the fifth century A.D., Germanic tribes and Mongol people called **Huns** invaded the Roman Empire. Romans referred to the Huns and Germanic tribes as **barbarians**, which then meant that they lived outside the empire. Eventually, the Huns conquered the Western Empire. The Eastern Empire survived for another thousand years.

REASONS FOR THE FALL OF ROME

1 There was no orderly way of choosing an emperor. It was often done by military leaders, who chose soldiers rather than effective rulers. The military often murdered emperors whom they didn't like.

2 To support the large army, Romans were heavily taxed. This created burdens for common people.

3 Small farmers could not compete with large landowners, who used slaves for labor. Less food was grown because of poor farming methods on estates.

4 People without jobs, such as out-of-work small farmers, used up tax money.

5 Diseases killed about a third of the people.

The Roman Empire was attacked by barbarian tribes during the fifth century A.D.

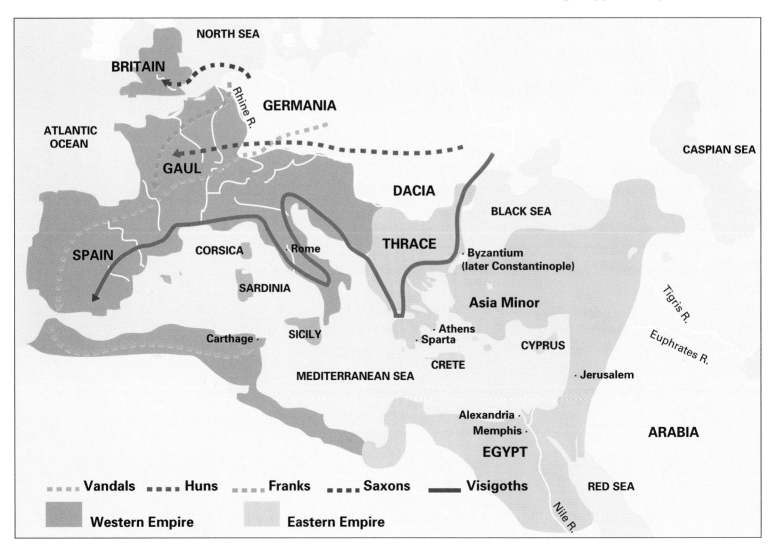

22

The Roman Gods

Roman gods were very much like Greek gods, but they had different names. Religion was the center of the Roman home and every family kept a shrine to the gods of the household—Janus and Vesta. Romans also built temples to their gods and goddesses.

Jupiter	The king of gods and god of light.
Juno	The queen of the gods.
Vesta	The goddess of the hearth.
Mars	The god of war.
Ceres	The goddess of the harvest and mother of the earth.
Minerva	The goddess of wisdom.
Venus	The goddess of love. Her son was Cupid.
Janus	The god of the beginnings. The first month of the year, January, is named for him.
Diana	The goddess of the moon and of hunting.
Neptune	The god of the sea.
Vulcan	The god of fire.
Mercury	The messenger of the gods and protector of traders.

The Beginnings of Christianity

During the reign of Augustus, a man named **Jesus** was born. He was a Jew who lived in Nazareth in the Roman province of Judea. Little is known about his childhood. All we know of Jesus comes from the Gospels of the New Testament in the Christian Bible. Jesus became a religious teacher with many followers. His followers called him Christ, which means "the anointed one." Jesus taught people to love God and their neighbors as much as they loved themselves. This teaching stressed the importance of forgiving people, living an unselfish life, and being sorry for your sins. The religion built on the teachings of Jesus became known as Christianity. It took hold as the Roman Empire was falling apart.

Roman officials believed Jesus was dangerous. He was arrested and put to death by crucifixion (fastened to a cross until he died). Despite the death of Jesus, Christianity grew and spread all over the Roman Empire. A number of Roman emperors tried to crush the religion. They put Christians in jail and even murdered them. This cruel punishment lasted for many years until the emperor Constantine became a Christian in A.D. 312 and made Christianity legal. Three centuries after the death of Jesus, Christianity became the main religion in the empire.

ACCOMPLISHMENTS OF THE ROMANS

1 They wrote a set of laws that became the basis of many legal systems for many countries of Europe and Latin America.

2 They built roads, bridges, and aqueducts to carry water. Building on the architecture developed by the Greeks, Roman architects built the arch, the dome, and the column. Some famous Roman buildings are the Temple of Vesta, the Pantheon, the Colosseum, the Theater of Pompey, and the Arch of Titus.

3 They created sculptures that actually looked like the people they portrayed, a first in ancient times.

4 Their language (Latin) became the basis for many other languages, including French, Italian, Spanish, and Portuguese.

5 The Roman poet Virgil wrote an epic poem, *The Aeneid*, which traces Rome's origins to Aeneas, one of the warriors in *The Iliad* by Homer (see p. 18).

6 They invented Roman numerals, which are still used today.

7 They united people and created peace in a vast empire.

Romans were excellent builders who incorporated arches, columns, and domes in their buildings. Even viaducts (bridges used to carry water) were designed using arches and columns.

The Seven Wonders of the Ancient World

The Seven Wonders of the Ancient World are famous buildings and statues from ancient history. The list was made by a Greek writer more than 2,000 years ago. Today, all have been destroyed or stand in ruins, except for the Egyptian pyramids.

The Colossus of Rhodes. A huge statue of the Greek god Helios that stood in the harbor of Rhodes in Greece. An earthquake destroyed it.

The Great Pyramids of Egypt. The magnificent tombs for the kings of Egypt.

The Mausoleum. Mausolus was a king in Asia Minor. Upon his death, his wife built him a monumental tomb at Halicarnassus.

The Temple of Artemis. The Greeks built this temple to the goddess Artemis at Ephesus. It was burned to the ground by an invading army.

The Hanging Gardens of Babylon. King Nebuchadnezzar II built these magnificent gardens with terraces. Water had to be pumped up to the top.

The Pharos Lighthouse. A huge lighthouse that was built in Egypt by the Greeks.

The Statue of Zeus. A beautiful statue of Zeus made of marble, ivory, and gold stood at Olympia in Greece.

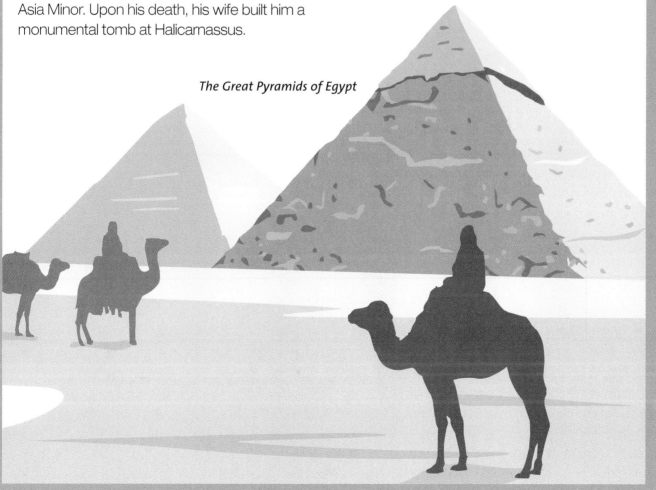

The Great Pyramids of Egypt

Asia
(3000 B.C.–A.D. 1900)

Ancient India and China

Like Egypt along the Nile River and the Mesopotamian civilizations along the Tigris and Euphrates rivers, early civilizations of Asia began along great rivers. The Indus River of India and the Yellow River in China were where they began. Asia has seen the rise and fall of many developed civilizations and great empires. The sites of these ancient cultures have grown to be the most populated places on Earth.

India (3000–1500 B.C.)

India is one of the oldest civilizations. It began more than 4,000 years ago, in an area known as the **Indus River Valley**. The main cities were Mohenjo-Daro and Harappa, and they were very much alike, even though they were 350 miles apart. Evidence of these ancient cities was found by archaeologists (people who study the life of ancient peoples) in the 1920s. They uncovered drainage and sewer systems, homes with bathrooms, large farms with irrigation canals, and many artifacts including jewelry, pottery, woven cloth, and tools and implements of copper and bronze.

What happened is a great mystery. Archaeologists are not sure, but a drought or flood may have wiped them out. Or people may have scattered after an invasion. They were gone by about 1500 B.C. The people who replaced them were nomads who herded animals. Hundreds of years went by before anyone built new cities in India.

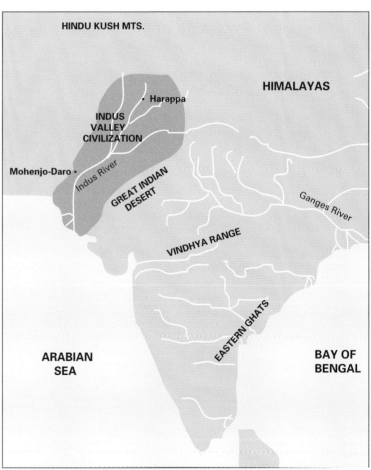

Indian civilization is believed to have begun in the Indus River Valley.

Hinduism

The nomadic people who entered northern India and the remaining scattered peoples of the Indus River cities formed a new culture in northern India. It was from this culture that the religion of Hinduism developed, beginning about 1500 B.C. Its special language was Sanskrit.

Hindus had thousands of gods and goddesses, and their priests sang from memory many long and complicated hymns to them. More than a thousand hymns were collected in the Hindu sacred text *Rig-Veda*.

Another sacred Hindu text, the *Upanishads*, was written about 400 B.C. In it, the basic ideas of Hinduism were collected:

- Brahman is the one great spirit, or supreme being.

- The Self, or Soul, called Atman, is a part of Brahman.

- Nothing living ever truly dies, and the spirit passes from one living thing to another. This is called reincarnation.

- All Hindus must seek perfect understanding, called moksha. In moksha, the self disappears and becomes one with Brahman.

THE CASTE SYSTEM

Closely tied to Hinduism was the caste system. People divided into four main groups, or castes:

- Priests (also called Brahmans) and scholars

- Warriors

- Merchants, farmers, and craftspeople

- Peasants and servants

People who did not belong to any group were called *untouchables*, and they were the lowest group of all. Indian Nationalist leader Mohandas Gandhi called them *Harijan*, which means "children of God." The caste system was outlawed in India in 1950, but many people still mix only with people of their caste.

The Indus Valley civilization grows up along the Indus River	Ancient China's rule by dynasties begins	Zhou dynasty	Confucius and Lao-tzu live during this period	Jesus lives during this period	The Golden Age of India begins	The powerful Mogul (Mongol) Empire begins	The Chinese Opium Wars	Japan is opened to trade
3000 B.C.	2000	1123–256	600–500	A.D. 1	320	1000	1839–1842	1853

Buddhism

A young man named **Siddhartha Gautama** was born near the Himalayan Mountains in Nepal about 563 B.C. Just before he became thirty years old, he left his wife and son and went away to find the meaning of life. After fasting and disciplining himself harshly, he was not satisfied. Finally, he meditated deeply under a tree. When he finished, he believed that the truth had been made known to him. He gave his first sermon to the five wisdom seekers who had journeyed with him, and from then on was known as **Buddha**, or "the enlightened one." He taught that suffering is brought on by people's desires, and that suffering can be ended — and complete happiness found — by ending all desires.

Buddha taught his followers to treat all living things with loving kindness. Buddhism appealed to people because it rejected the caste system and treated everyone — women and men, rich and poor — with respect. It was taught in the everyday language of the people, not in Sanskrit.

Later, Buddhism spread to China and Japan but nearly died out in India.

ACCOMPLISHMENTS OF THE ANCIENT INDIANS

1 They founded the Hindu religion. Hinduism is one of the chief religions in India today.

2 They originated the Buddhist religion. Buddhism rejected the caste system promoted by Hinduism.

3 They further developed art and architecture, especially of temples.

4 They wrote fine literature, particularly in Sanskrit, including fables, stories, and poems. Sacred texts include the Rig-Veda.

Image of Buddha

THE MAURYAN EMPIRE

The Mauryan Empire, from about 321 to 185 B.C., was the first to unite most of India under a central government. Its center was along the Ganges River and its capital was Pataliputra. Great rulers of the Mauryan Empire were **Chandragupta** and **A´soka**.

Chandragupta came to power in 322 B.C. and ruled until 298 B.C. With his army of 70,000 soldiers, 9,000 elephants, and 10,000 chariots, he conquered northern and central India, as well as what is today western Pakistan and part of Afghanistan. He was a stern ruler, but his empire prospered.

A´soka, the grandson of Chandragupta, ruled from about 264 to 223 B.C. He guided India into a period of peace. A religious ruler, A soka sent missionaries into other countries to spread the message of Buddha. He also established hospitals, forbade animal sacrifices, and urged vegetarianism. A´soka was regarded as a kind and noble ruler.

THE GUPTA EMPIRE

Hundreds of years after the first Chandragupta died, another Indian ruler took his name. The Gupta Empire was begun by **Chandra Gupta I** in A.D. 320. He was the first of many rulers of his family who reigned over the empire until A.D. 500. The Guptas originally ruled a small kingdom in northeast India, but eventually their empire came to include all of northern India and parts of central and southern India. Like the Mauryan Empire before it, the capital was Pataliputra on the Ganges River.

After the Guptas took control, they restored law and order and people began to prosper again. The Gupta reign came to be known as the **Golden Age of India**.

Under the Gupta Empire, people followed both the Buddhist and Hindu religions (see pp. 27–28). The Gupta Empire ended when Muslim Turks invaded from Central Asia. The Golden Age of India had come to an end, and a new religion was brought to India.

ACCOMPLISHMENTS DURING THE GOLDEN AGE OF INDIA

1 Medical doctors set broken bones, used plastic surgery to repair ears and noses, and gave the first shots to prevent diseases.

2 Mathematicians invented the decimal (base-ten) number system and the Arabic numerals that are still in use today (1 to 9). They also developed the idea of zero and the concept of infinity, or endlessness, represented by the symbol ∞.

3 Great books and epics (stories told in long poems) were created, such as the *Mahabharata*, *Ramayana*, and the *Bhagavad Gita*.

4 Artists, musicians, and dancers flourished. They developed classical dances and music still enjoyed today.

5 Textiles were created from slender threads, including cashmere, calico, and chintz.

MOGUL (MONGOL) EMPIRE

Muslims began to invade India between A.D. 1000 and the 1500s. The Muslims were followers of a religion called **Islam**. Muslims believed that people were created equal, and that anyone can improve his or her social status by hard work. This was a very different belief from the one that put forth the Hindu caste system and caused many conflicts between Hindus and Muslims.

The word **Mogul** comes from the Persian-Indian word for Mongol. The Mogul Empire was founded in 1526 when **Babur**, the Mogul ruler of Afghanistan, conquered India and united it with Afghanistan.

The most renowned Mogul leader was **Akbar**, whose name means "great." He was the grandson of Babur and only thirteen years old when he became king in 1556. He ruled for forty-nine years, until 1605. Akbar expanded the empire's territories and provided a strong central government. During his rule, India became one of the leading centers of culture. Musicians, dancers, artists, and poets were invited to produce great works. Some of the most magnificent **mosques** (places of Muslim worship) were built during this period. This includes perhaps the most famous Indian monument, the Taj Mahal, built by **Shah Jahan** as a tomb for his wife. Akbar was also a just ruler who treated Hindus as equals of Muslims. He removed taxes on non-Muslims and forbade taking Hindus as slaves. He is considered one of history's finest rulers.

The last ruler of the Mogul Empire, **'Alam-gír**, ruled from 1658 to 1707. He tried to force Hindus to become Muslims. He taxed non-Muslims and would not permit them to build Hindu temples. This led to many revolts. A group called the Rajputs successfully fought the Muslims and saved Hinduism in northern India. The kingdom became weak and broke into smaller states. Muslims had great influence upon India.

Muslim Influences upon India

- ❖ **Government.** Muslims became the ruling class over the more numerous Hindus.
- ❖ **Religion.** Islam grew in India and hostility between the Hindus and Muslims also increased. Muslims remained a distinctly separate group from the larger population of Hindus.
- ❖ **Language.** Arabic and Persian languages were introduced. Persian was the official language of the Mogul Empire. Over time, the Persian and Hindi languages formed into a new language, called Urdu.
- ❖ **Architecture.** Muslims built many palaces, mosques, and other monuments using arches and domes. Muslim architecture was much simpler than the ornate Hindu architecture.

BRITISH RULE IN INDIA

The Portuguese explorer **Vasco da Gama** was probably the first European to reach India. Trade routes were soon established with England, France, and Denmark. In the 1600s, the British East India Company built trading posts in Calcutta, Bombay, and Madras. As the Mogul Empire weakened, the East India Company began controlling territories. By the late 1700s, Great Britain had become India's most powerful ruler, overthrowing Indian rebellions as well as French attempts at control. The English gained complete control of India, and in 1877 announced Queen Victoria of England to be the Empress of India.

By the 1800s, Britain was the world's largest **imperial** power. Imperialism exists when one country tries to extend its power and control over another. India became Britain's largest and most productive colony. For this reason, India was often called the Jewel in the Crown. The British made great profits from industries, such as textiles, in India, which they shipped back to England. As a result, however, the British destroyed India's own economy.

The British made a number of improvements in India. They stopped local wars and built railroads, highways, hospitals, and a telegraph system. By developing industry, they created jobs. On the other hand, the population grew so fast that the demand for jobs could not be filled. Most Indians lived close to starvation and paid high rents and taxes. The English lived far better than the Indians and kept themselves segregated (separated).

The Fight for Independence

Mohandas Gandhi

Eventually the Indians began to revolt. When the British passed laws in 1919 that forbade Indians to hold group meetings, 2,000 people, led by **Mohandas Gandhi**, gathered in a town square at Amritsar. British soldiers killed nearly 400 unarmed men, women, and children. Gandhi called for a nationwide nonviolent protest and urged Indians to refuse to obey the British. He called this **passive resistance**. His followers refused to buy British goods, pay taxes, or work for the government, and they disregarded British law. Gandhi was put in jail for two years, yet the independence movement still gained force. Finally, the British gave in and began to talk about granting India limited self-government. A long struggle for independence finally succeeded in 1947, when the modern nations of India and Pakistan were formed. One of Gandhi's followers, **Jawaharlal Nehru**, became India's first prime minister, and India became the world's largest democracy.

China

Chinese civilization grew up along two large rivers. The first was called the Huang He, which means Yellow River. In the Yellow River Valley, people farmed rice, soybeans, barley, and wheat. Many villages were walled to protect them from invaders. Each of the small villages had its own government. The second river was the Chang Jiang, or Long River, in the southern part of China. It was so powerful that it cut deep gorges through the Asian mountains.

THE RULE OF DYNASTIES

Ancient China's history is divided into dynasties and dates back to 2000 B.C. A **dynasty** is a succession of rulers from the same family. The Chinese believed that their rulers were divinely selected. They called this process the **Mandate of Heaven**. The Chinese had eleven major dynasties before a revolution put an end to the last emperor in 1911.

Major Chinese dynasties from 1500 B.C. to A.D. 222

The Teachings of Confucius

Confucius lived from 551 to 479 B.C. His teachings had great influence on the people of China. During his lifetime, he traveled all over China to instruct people about his ideas. He wanted to improve society and achieve good government. He taught that the following virtues are guidelines to a happy and useful life:

- **There are five relationships that need to be obeyed: between ruler and subject, father and son, husband and wife, older brother and younger brother, friend and friend.**

- **Be sincere, polite, and unselfish.**

- **Obey and respect laws and traditions.**

- **Work hard and respect learning.**

Early Chinese Dynasties

DYNASTY	CULTURE	ART	RELIGION & PHILOSOPHY	FAMOUS LEADERS
HSIA 2000–1500 B.C.	millet and wheat cultivated potter's wheel used animals domesticated	black pottery		
SHANG 1500–1122 B.C.	writing invented silkworms cultivated for silk the wheel used on war chariots	white pottery fine bronze worked marble and ivory carved jade and turquoise used	belief in spirit world filial piety ancestor worship	
ZHOU 1123–256 B.C.	astronomy advanced crossbow invented	lacquer	Confucianism Taoism	
CH'IN 221–206 B.C.	Great Wall built		Legalism official policy	Ch'in Shih took title Huang Ti, meaning "emperor"
HAN 202 B.C.–A.D. 222	iron sword used soybean cultivated	wall painting sculpture	Confucianism official policy	

Later Chinese Dynasties

DYNASTY	CULTURE	ART	FAMOUS LEADERS
SUI A.D. 589–618	Grand Canal built		Yang Ti
T'ANG A.D. 618–906	building of schools	golden age of poetry, literature, art, music	Wu Chao, first female emperor
SUNG A.D. 960–1279	inventions of magnetic compass, paper money, book printing	golden age of painting porcelain	
YUAN/MONGOL A.D. 1279–1368	increase in trade abroad use of gunpowder as a weapon		Genghis Khan Kublai Khan
MING A.D. 1368–1644	Forbidden City built Yung-lo Encyclopedia of Chinese writings Grand Fleet makes China an international naval power		Chu Yuan-Chang
MANCHU A.D. 1644–1911			Empress Dowager Tz'u-hsi

The Opium Wars (1839–1842)

Because the Chinese would not trade with Western nations, the British smuggled opium from India into China. Many Chinese became addicted to the illegal drug, which made them unable to work. The Chinese government tried to stop the trade of this habit-forming drug, but their laws were not obeyed. In 1839, Chinese troops destroyed millions of dollars' worth of British opium. This led to the Opium Wars and three years of fighting between China and England.

The British won easily, and in 1842 a peace treaty was signed. The Treaty of Nanking gave the island of Hong Kong, off the southern coast of China, to England. Another result of the treaty was the opening of five Chinese ports to foreign trade.

Taoism

Taoism comes from the word **Tao**, which means the Way, or the Path, to happiness. Its founder was **Lao-tzu**, a philosopher who lived during the time of Confucius but who believed people should lead simple and natural lives in harmony with nature. By understanding nature's way, people will achieve inner peace. The supposed author of the *Tao-te Ching*, Lao-tzu encouraged people to meditate (to think quietly) about nature's way, and to be content with what they had—not to reach for fame or fortune. He also believed that there should be no interference from government.

THE EMPRESS DOWAGER AND THE END OF CHINESE DYNASTIES

The Empress Dowager was the ruler of China from 1861 to her death in 1908. Her name was **Tz'u-hsi**. She became one of the most powerful women in the history of China. Though ruthless, she abolished the centuries-old practice of foot binding, a custom that left girls and women permanently crippled.

During her reign, foreigners were taking control over parts of China. The Chinese resented this, and eventually the empress also supported the anti-foreigner rebels known as the Boxers. This secret society attacked foreigners in many parts of the country. In 1900 the Boxer rebellion reached its peak. Western nations and Japan banded together and defeated the Boxers. Tz'u-hsi was forced to flee Beijing, and China was forced to pay millions of dollars in damages, which put the nation in debt. Tz'u-hsi returned in 1902, though in 1911, a revolution led by **Sun Yat-sen** made China a republic. This ended 267 years of Manchu rule.

After the 1911 rebellion, a China Republic was declared in 1912. The first president was Sun Yat-sen. He founded the Kuomintang (Nationalist party) and began to modernize China. The Communist party was organized in 1921, with **Mao Zedong** as its leader. The Communist party joined forces with the Nationalist party, under the leadership of **Chiang Kai-shek**, in order to try to reunite China. Differences between the two parties led to a civil war, resulting in the deaths of many Communists. However, when the Japanese launched a war against China in 1937, the two groups joined together again to fight the Japanese until World War II ended in 1945. The unity did not last. In 1946, fighting between Communists and Nationalists began in Manchuria. Communists gained control of China by October 1949, and Nationalists withdrew to Taiwan.

MAO ZEDONG

Attracted to the nationalist ideas of Sun Yat-sen, **Mao Zedong** joined the army when he was eighteen and fought in the revolution that overthrew the Manchu dynasty in 1911. Several years later, while studying at Peking (Beijing) University, he came across the teachings of Karl Marx, and committed his life to the ideas of socialism. Eventually, he became the leader of the Communist revolution and then chairman of the People's Republic of China (P.R.C.) from 1949 to 1959. Mao remained chairman of the Communist party until his death in 1976.

Chinese calligraphy is read from top to bottom: children's encyclopedia.

Japan

Very little is known of Japan's history before the sixth century A.D. because there were no written records. Historians believe that the earliest people, called **Jomon**, lived by fishing and hunting on Honshu Island between 8000 and 300 B.C. About 200 B.C., the Jomon were replaced by the **Yayoi**. The Yayoi cultivated rice and irrigated the land. The Japanese had now become farmers.

Around A.D. 300, the Japanese came under a loose form of government known as **Yamato**. The Yamato period lasted about 300 years. Korean and Chinese culture, including Buddhism, was introduced. The ruler in 607 was **Prince Shotoku Taishi**. He sent students to China, the most advanced civilization of the time, to study its culture. As a result, the Japanese borrowed many things from the Chinese, including written characters, arts, mathematics, architecture, and agricultural techniques.

THE HEIAN PERIOD (A.D. 794–1185)

In 794, **Emperor Kammu** made the city of Heian (present-day Kyoto) the capital of Japan. The city's name means "peace and tranquility." The Fujiwara family came to power in 858. They ruled Japan for 300 years. The Fujiwara era was a time of refinement and luxury and came to be known as the Heian Period. The arts flourished and writing and poetry became popular.

Two of the most important writers of this period were **Lady Murasaki Shikibu** and **Lady Sei Shonagon**. Lady Murasaki wrote *The Tale of Genji*, the world's first novel. The story was about the upper class of Japan.

THE RISE OF SHOGUNS IN THE FEUDAL AGE

Landowners in the country had created large estates and ruled them according to their own sets of laws, rather than the emperor's. The lords, or landowners, were given land by small farmers who, in turn, received their lord's protection from other warring lords. The exchange of land in return for service or protection is called **feudalism**. The great lords were called **daimyo**. They hired lesser lords to fight for them, called **samurai**. The samurai warriors fought for the lords and had to be absolutely loyal to them. They lived by a code of behavior called **bushido**, or "the way of the warrior." This was a strict code of absolute obedience. The samurai were rewarded with land and wealth, but were expected to die for their lords if necessary.

The central Heian government grew too weak to control the countryside. Two clans — the Taira and Minamoto — fought for control. The Minamoto took control. A military leader named **Yoritomo** led the new government. In 1192, Yoritomo was given the title **shogun**, which means "the emperor's general." The emperor remained at Kyoto, but the shogun Yoritomo ruled Japan from Kamakura, near present-day Tokyo. This system of government — in which Japan was ruled by military governments called **shogunates** — lasted for almost 700 years.

The major shogunates were the Kamakura Shogunate (1192–1333), the Ashikaga Shogunate (1338–1573), and the Tokugawa Shogunate (1600–1867).

Samurai armor is made of steel, silk, and bronze.

ISOLATION

Between 1200 and 1600, there were many civil wars. In 1600, when the **Tokugawa** Shogunate came to power, it united Japan once again. In order to keep unity, the Tokugawa wanted all foreigners to leave Japan. In 1640, the shogunate expelled all foreigners, outlawed Christianity, and greatly reduced trade. No Japanese were allowed to leave the country. This began a period of isolation that lasted for 200 years.

MEIJI RESTORATION (1868–1912)

Many Japanese were outraged over treaties the shogun made with Westerners. The samurai in southern Japan began attacking European ships and a full rebellion began. The Tokugawa family shogun ruled for 200 years until many Japanese became outraged over treaties. In 1867, the rebels overthrew the Tokugawa Shogunate. In 1868, a fifteen-year-old prince was named emperor. He took the name Meiji, meaning "enlightened rule." This signified the return, or restoration, of the emperor's rule.

Meiji leaders began to Westernize, or adopt ways of Western countries of Europe and North America. They eliminated the positions of shogun, daimyo, and samurai. Students and officials were sent to Europe and America to study Western education, science, government, and military organization. The Japanese government built railroads, industries, and telegraph lines. In fewer than thirty-five years after the Meiji became emperor, Japan had built a modern, strong empire.

The Opening of Japan

In 1853, Commodore **Matthew Perry** of the United States came to Japan. Perry wanted a trade agreement. He brought four warships and a large force. This strong military show both impressed and frightened the Japanese. They gave Perry the trade treaty he wanted. Japan soon signed similar trade agreements with other Western nations. Isolation had been broken.

ACCOMPLISHMENTS OF THE EARLY JAPANESE

1 Although they originally borrowed from the Chinese, the early Japanese gradually built their own culture. For example, Chinese written characters were used to write the Japanese language.

2 They developed literature and poetry, including the writing of the world-famous novel *The Tale of Genji*.

3 They developed the Shinto religion, a form of nature worship. Ancestor worship also developed.

4 They placed great emphasis on good manners and a love of beauty.

The Byzantine and Muslim Empires (A.D. 527–1932)

Ancient Middle East Roots

There were two great empires in the Middle East—the Christian Byzantine and the Muslim. Both were rivals for control of the Middle East. The Byzantine Empire thrived in present-day Turkey. The Muslim Empire centered on the Arabian Peninsula in present-day Saudi Arabia. Except for religion, these two empires had a great deal in common in their ways of life.

The Byzantine Empire

The Byzantine Empire was the Roman Empire of the east. One of Rome's great emperors was **Constantine,** who moved the capital of the Roman Empire to the city of Byzantium (see p. 21). He renamed the capital Constantinople (now Istanbul, Turkey), and it became the center of the Byzantine Empire. As the western half of Rome declined, the Byzantine Empire grew and became very wealthy from trade. Constantinople also became a great center of Christianity. Constantine had converted to the Christian faith and he encouraged Christian scholars to come and study.

Justinian was a great army general and one of the greatest Byzantine emperors. Together with his wife, **Theodora**, he ruled from A.D. 527 to 565. Justinian expanded westward to recapture much of the Western Empire of Rome, including northern Africa, southern Spain, and Italy. He also instituted a new set of laws called the **Justinian Code**. These laws were based on the Roman laws. They were strict but fair, and gave the same rights to everyone, rich or poor. This code of laws became a model for lawmakers all over western Europe.

Constantine

The Byzantine Empire is ruled by Justinian and Theodora The Justinian Code becomes law	Muhammad leads Muslims from Mecca to Medina Islam spreads throughout the Muslim Empire	Basil II becomes emperor of Byzantium and the empire enters the Byzantine Golden Age	Süleyman the Magnificent rules the great Ottoman Empire	The kingdom of Saudi Arabia is formed
A.D. 527–565	622	976	1520–1566	1932

38

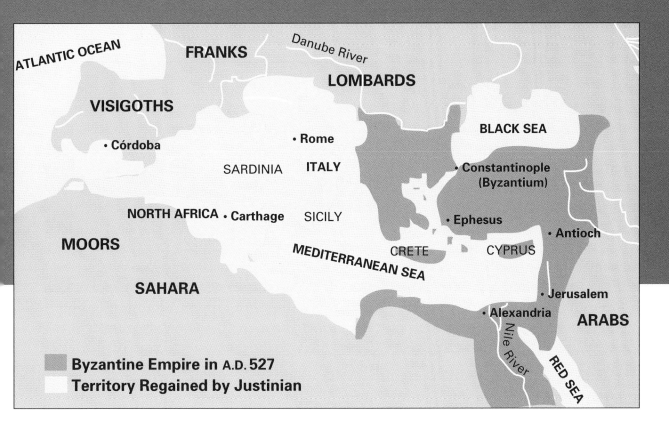

Byzantine Empire in A.D. 527
Territory Regained by Justinian

In 976, **Basil II** became emperor. He expanded the empire and made it even more powerful and wealthy. The empire entered the **Byzantine Golden Age**. Artists, musicians, and architects thrived. Poets and historians wrote great works during this period. Education was stressed and new universities were built. Parks, playgrounds, museums, and libraries were built for the people. It was a time of great achievement.

The Byzantine Empire declined gradually from the 1000s to the 1400s, when it was constantly invaded by enemies. The Muslim Turks conquered Asian sections of the empire in 1071. Then Roman Catholics from western Europe began a series of wars called the **Crusades** (see also p. 74), eventually sacking the wealthy city of Constantinople in 1204. The Byzantine Empire ended in 1453 when the Ottoman Turks captured Constantinople.

ACCOMPLISHMENTS OF THE BYZANTINES

1 They helped preserve Greek and Roman culture by keeping alive the plays, poems, and ideas of the ancient Western world. The West (Europe) couldn't do this because during this time, most Europeans could not read.

2 They followed Roman laws, passing them on to western Europe.

3 They spread Christianity into eastern Europe, including Russia, Bulgaria, and Bosnia. Missionaries taught people how to read and write.

The Muslim Empire

By the eighth century, the Muslim Empire was the largest and most populated of its time. Its boundaries extended from India to Spain (see map p. 41). The first capital was at Damascus, and later at Baghdad. Its people were **Arabs**, who came from Arabia.

The Islamic religion of the Muslim Empire was founded by the prophet **Muhammad** in the seventh century. Muhammad was born in the city of Mecca in Arabia. He had a vision that he was to become God's messenger. He began to teach that there is only one God, called **Allah** (the Arabic word for God). Because many people thought Muhammad dangerous, he fled for his life to the city of Medina, where people accepted his teachings. Muhammad's flight is called the **Hegira**. The year of his flight, 622, is the first year of the Muslim calendar.

THE SPREAD OF ISLAM

In 630, Muhammad's army captured Mecca. Muhammad destroyed the statues of the other religions and set out to unify the peoples of Arabia. He conquered many other areas, and the Muslim Empire began to grow. Islam spread quickly. After Muhammad's death in 632, **Abū Bakr** convinced Muhammad's followers to continue his work. Abū Bakr became the first **caliph**, a religious leader and head of the Muslim state. His armies conquered the Persian Empire and much of the Byzantine Empire. Muslim armies then took North Africa and marched to the Atlantic Ocean. The Muslims did not force people to convert to Islam and allowed all religions to be practiced. However, Muslims paid lower taxes and were able to keep their land.

The **Umayyad** caliphs gained power in 661, after the murder of the fourth caliph, **'Ali**. Muslims who supported 'Ali refused to recognize the Umayyad caliphs. This led to a revolt. Eventually, in 750, a new family of caliphs, called the Abbasids, took over. Their capital was **Baghdad**. The rule of the Abbasids lasted until 1055. During this time the greatest expansion of Islam took place. By the tenth century, Islam dominated a large part of the world.

The Muslim Empire gradually declined, and by the eleventh century, the empire had been divided into a number of independent kingdoms. The family of **Seljuk** conquered the Abbasids and created their own empire. In 1258, the Mongols defeated the Seljuks. They were not Muslims and destroyed much of the Muslim culture. By 1453, the Ottoman Turks had established a new Muslim Empire that would last into the twentieth century.

The Teachings of Muhammad

Islam is the religion based on the teachings of the prophet Muhammad. These teachings are written down in Islam's holy book, the Koran (also spelled Qur'an). The Koran sets down five obligations to guide the lives of all Muslims. These five obligations are:

1. **To confess that there is no God but Allah, and Muhammad is His Prophet.**
2. **To pray five times a day.**
3. **To treat all Muslims as brothers and sisters and to give to the poor.**
4. **To not eat between sunrise and sunset in the holy month of Ramadan.**
5. **To make a pilgrimage to Mecca at least once, if possible.**

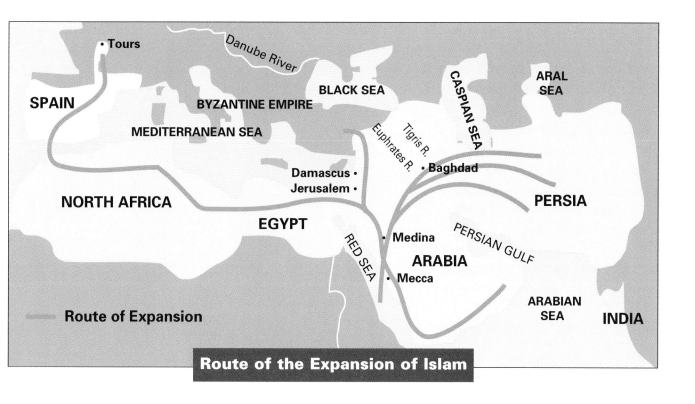

Route of the Expansion of Islam

ACCOMPLISHMENTS OF THE MUSLIMS

1 They founded great universities, especially in Egypt, Baghdad, and Spain. They built many libraries and schools.

2 They brought the use of zero and Arabic numerals (adopted from India) to their empire. They also made advances in algebra and geometry.

3 They used chemicals to make medicines, began performing surgery, and wrote medical textbooks, including the famous *Book of Healing* and the *Canon of Medicine* by Avicenna.

4 Astronomers kept records of the heavens and scientists studied the properties of light.

5 Great literary works, including *The Rubáiyát* by Omar Khayyám, were produced.

Today there are two groups of Muslims. Sunni Muslims are the larger group. They believe that the only source of Islam is the Koran. The smaller group are called Shiite Muslims. They accept that there are three sources of Islam — the Koran, Muhammad, and 'Ali's descendants. They also believe that only the descendants of 'Ali can lawfully rule the Islamic community.

The Ottoman Empire

The founder of the Ottoman Empire was **Osman**. He was head of a Turkish group who called themselves Osmanlis, or "sons of Osman." These people later became known as Ottomans. Osman and his son, **Orkhan**, captured most of the Byzantine Empire. Orkhan was the first Ottoman leader to become a **sultan**, the Turkish name for emperor. Osman and his son were never able to capture Constantinople. In 1453, Sultan **Mehmet II** captured the city and rebuilt it. He ordered that Hagia Sophia, the largest Christian church, be turned into a **mosque**, or Muslim place of worship. The former Christian capital now became the center of an Islamic empire.

By the sixteenth century, the Ottomans had enormous power under Sultan Süleyman I, also known as **Süleyman the Magnificent**, who ruled from 1520 to 1566. He greatly expanded the empire to include southern Russia and the Balkans and much of North Africa. The eastern lands extended to the Persian Gulf. During his rule, the Ottoman Empire reached its greatest heights in military power and culture. Süleyman reformed the educational and legal systems and encouraged the arts and sciences. Great mosques, schools, bridges, and monuments were built.

The military skill of the Ottomans was partly due to the drafting of Christians into a special army corps called the **Janissaries**. These highly trained foot soldiers were rewarded with positions in the army and government.

The Ottoman Empire weakened greatly in the eighteenth and nineteenth centuries. In 1826, Sultan **Mahmud II** eliminated the Janissaries because they had so much power. He gradually westernized the empire. This did not stop the decline. A group called the **Young Turks** overthrew Sultan **Abdülhamid II** in 1909.

Janissaries could be recognized by their elaborate headdresses.

Africa
(2000 B.C.–Present)

Chapter 1 The Kush

Kush was the land south of Egypt (see p. 11) in present-day Sudan. Its people, also called the Kush, lived along the Nile River from about 2000 B.C. to A.D. 350. They were farmers and cattle raisers. They also mined gold and copper. The Kush were conquered and ruled by the Egyptians for thousands of years. The Egyptians went to Kush and took gold, ebony, ivory, cattle, and slaves back to Egypt. Many Egyptians came to live in Kush and the Kush began to worship the same gods. Their priests used Egyptian hieroglyphics to write.

When the Egyptian Empire weakened around 1100 B.C., the Kush became independent. They built a great army and, in 752 B.C., invaded and conquered Egypt. The Kush ruled Egypt for nearly one hundred years before they were conquered by the Assyrians (see p. 5).

After their defeat, the Kush moved their capital to Meroe. They realized they had lost Egypt because the Assyrians had iron weapons. The people of Meroe began to use iron. They made weapons and farm tools. Meroe became one of the biggest iron-making cities of the ancient world. It was from Kush that the knowledge of iron making spread south and west.

The Kush were defeated by the king and army of **Axum** about A.D. 350. After this, the Kush disappeared.

Leather, plant fiber, and wood were used to make this mask used in religious dances.

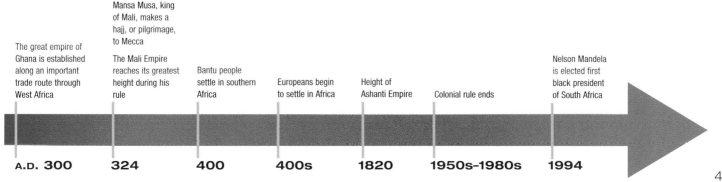

The great empire of Ghana is established along an important trade route through West Africa

Mansa Musa, king of Mali, makes a hajj, or pilgrimage, to Mecca

The Mali Empire reaches its greatest height during his rule

Bantu people settle in southern Africa

Europeans begin to settle in Africa

Height of Ashanti Empire

Colonial rule ends

Nelson Mandela is elected first black president of South Africa

A.D. 300   324   400   400s   1820   1950s–1980s   1994

Chapter 2

Early African Empires

Ghana

The first great empire in West Africa was that of the wealthy and mighty Ghana. The heart of the Ghanian Empire lay west of Kush, on the western edge of the vast grasslands of north-central Africa known as the Sudan. The **Soninkes** were among the first peoples to live in this region, from about A.D. 300 to 500.

The people of Ghana lived along an important trade route. To the south of Ghana was a large forest. To the north was the Sahara Desert. Ghana became a wealthy nation by controlling the roads and charging taxes for trade between the people of the forest and the people of the desert.

The people of the desert were called **Berbers**. They were traders who crossed the deserts in caravans, or large groups. The Berber traders exchanged salt and mined in the desert for gold. Later, Ghana also traded with Arabs who invaded North Africa.

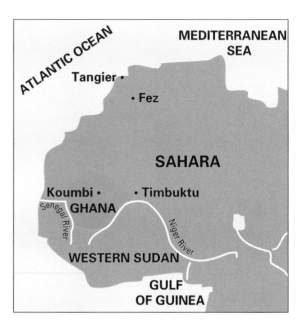

Gold, iron, and important trade routes brought about the rise of Ghana, in purple, in the area of West Africa known as the Sudan.

Two metals played an important role in the development of Ghana—gold and iron. Ghana itself had few natural resources, but it became wealthy by controlling trade and acting as go-between for gold and salt that were exchanged in its territory. Iron was important because it allowed the people of Ghana to make and trade swords, daggers, arrows, and other weapons. This gave Ghana's warriors great advantage over their enemies.

The kingdom of Ghana first rose to power around A.D. 700 and disappeared around 1200. The capital city was Koumbi, and it had around 15,000 people. Koumbi was conquered and destroyed in 1076 by Berber Muslims known as **Almoravids**. They built a great empire in northwest Africa and northern Spain.

Other invaders attacked Ghana as well. The Arab Muslims tried to force the Ghanians to convert to their religion many times. In 1203, Ghana was attacked by the **Sosso** tribe. After that, Ghana became weak and powerless.

ACCOMPLISHMENTS OF THE GHANIANS

1 They established important trade routes.

2 They controlled the gold and salt trade.

3 They controlled roads and charged taxes for passage, creating a wealthy nation.

Mali

Mali succeeded Ghana as the major kingdom in the western Sudan. The empire of Mali contained the former Ghana as well as much more territory.

The power shift began when **Sumanguru**, the leader of the Sosso tribe, destroyed Ghana in 1203. There was a power struggle between the Sosso and the **Mandingo** people, led by **Sundiata**. The Mandingo defeated the Sosso in 1235 and went on to found the Mali Empire. There is a legend that tells of Sumanguru vanishing during the battle and a giant baobab tree springing up at the spot. Descendants still claim Sundiata as their great national hero.

The capital of Mali was Kangaba on the Niger River. After Sundiata defeated Sumanguru, he moved the capital to Niani. Islam was the major religion. The kingdom of Mali became a key region in the Islamic world of the Middle Ages. The rulers were called **mansa**, which means "emperor" or "sultan." **Mansa Musa**, a descendent of Sundiata, was the most famous ruler in the history of the western Sudan. He became mansa in 1312 and ruled for twenty-five years. Mansa Musa extended the boundaries of his empire, promoted trade and commerce, and encouraged the spread of learning. He also loved the arts, including paintings, architecture, and literature. He was devoutly religious.

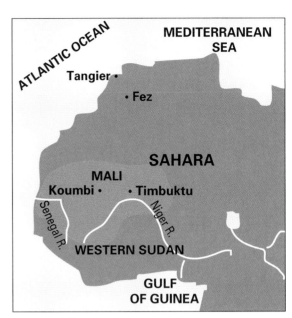

The Mali kingdom, outlined in purple.

Mansa Musa made a pilgrimage to Mecca, the holy city of Islam. Such a pilgrimage is called a **hajj**, and is part of the five basic observances of the Islamic religion (see p. 40). Mansa Musa's pilgrimage was one of the grandest of all times. He spread his wealth throughout the cities he passed. Mansa Musa became famous and many people traveled to his kingdom. He died in 1337.

Mali maintained an enormous army to keep peace within its empire, believed to have been more than 100,000 men. Mali's main crops were sorghum, rice, taro, yams, beans, cotton, and onions. People raised poultry, cattle, sheep, and goats. Mali replaced Ghana as the greatest power of the western Sudan, taking over the trans-Saharan gold and salt trade.

The Mali Empire was at its largest under Mansa Musa's rule, but after his death, the empire began to decline. By the end of the fifteenth century, it had dwindled to a small, unimportant state.

ACCOMPLISHMENTS OF THE MALIANS

1 They established trade and commerce throughout their empire.

2 They promoted learning and education.

3 They received fame through Mansa Musa's hajj.

The Songhai

The Songhai resisted the rule of the Mali and built their own empire around the mid-1400s. They were river people who lived along the Niger. Gao was their capital. Another great city was Timbuktu, which became a center of Islamic learning and a large trading center, with more than 50,000 people.

The earliest Songhai were mainly farmers and fishermen. They first settled in a town called Kukya, which became their capital. Around the eighth century, the Berber nomads captured Kukya and the Songhai moved further north to a new town that became Gao. By the eleventh century, the leader of Songhai had converted to Islam. For the next 300 years, the Songhai were constantly trying to remain free of Mali rule.

One of their fiercest warrior kings was **Sunni Ali Ber**. He came to the throne in 1464, recapturing the city of Timbuktu and later capturing the city of Jenne, another important trading center. Many thought him cruel, but he was highly regarded by his own people. Sunni Ali Ber was an able ruler with a talent for organization and government. He divided his empire into provinces and placed governors in control. He understood the importance of the Niger River in commerce and in military operations. Around 1475, Songhai replaced its rival, Mali, as the dominant power in the western Sudan. Sunni Ali Ber died in 1492 after ruling for nearly twenty-eight years.

ACCOMPLISHMENTS OF THE SONGHAI

1 They established a great center of Islamic learning in the empire.

2 They encouraged skilled craftspeople and artisans.

3 They built and maintained a large army.

The Songhai Empire, outlined in purple, was established after the Mali Empire declined. The Songhai built a great center for trade and Islamic learning at Timbuktu, in the heart of the salt caravan routes from the Sahara to the Atlantic coast.

The Dogon, also known as "people of the cliffs," have lived in Mali since the early Mali Empire of the twelfth century.

The Zanj

The people of Zanj lived on the eastern coast of Africa, from present-day Mozambique to Kenya, and on the island of Madagascar. They were mostly traders, exchanging ivory for wheat, rice, sesame oil, cotton, and honey. They also exported gold, tortoise shells, and slaves. The Zanj had been trading with China, Arabia, and India for almost 2,000 years when the Portuguese discovered them in the late 1400s. Between 1200 and 1500, trade with China, their farthest commercial partner, was extensive.

The people of Zanj built beautiful towns and were very good craftspeople. When the Portuguese arrived, they looted, destroyed towns, and killed citizens. Ruins and pottery fragments are the only things that exist from this lost kingdom.

ACCOMPLISHMENTS OF THE ZANJ

1 They established trade farther from home than any other African peoples.

2 They were skilled craftspeople and builders.

Zimbabwe

A number of **Bantu** peoples (speakers of the ancient language of Bantu) moved from West Africa to the area between the Zambezi and Limpopo rivers in southern Africa. Beginning around A.D. 400, they began mining for gold in the hills around the rivers. They took the gold to the Indian Ocean where they traded it for cloth, glass beads, and other goods. Around 1100, one group of these people began constructing thick stone-walled buildings. The area encompassing these buildings became the capital of an important kingdom called Zimbabwe. Zimbabwe means "great stone houses."

The builders of Zimbabwe were very skillful. The structures they built were sturdier and higher than those of other kingdoms. Neither mortar nor square corners were used, yet the stones fit together perfectly. They built a great stone city.

Zimbabwe became wealthy from its gold and ivory trade. The people were ruled by kings and were protected by a powerful army. Their empire lasted until the 1800s, when the last king was killed. The current nation of Zimbabwe took its name from these great Zimbabwe ruins when it became independent from Great Britain in 1980.

ACCOMPLISHMENTS OF THE ZIMBABWEANS

1 They mined gold for trade and established a large gold and ivory trade.

2 They were excellent builders, especially with stone.

Even without mortar, these 800-foot-long granite walls in Zimbabwe stand thirty-two feet high.

The European Colonization of Africa

Chapter 3

In the mid-1400s, the Portuguese began sailing from the Iberian Peninsula of Europe to the west coast of Africa. Prince **Henry the Navigator** encouraged the establishment of a number of trading posts along the west coast. The Portuguese were followed by the Dutch in the seventeenth century. During the 1800s, other Europeans moved into Africa. They took control of the continent, sometimes by force, and set up colonies. This became known as **colonial rule**.

The Industrial Revolution (see pp. 88–89) had given Europeans the ability to make weapons that were better than any made in Africa. Inventions such as the steam engine, the telegraph, and the railroad gave Europeans the means to build empires. Europeans saw these developments as proof that they had the right to rule people who were not industrialized. They were often convinced that it was their duty as Christians to spread their religion, too.

Ten percent of the African continent was under direct European control by 1875, and by 1900 most of Africa was ruled by six European powers — France, Great Britain, Portugal, Germany, Belgium, and Italy. These were the major areas they settled and controlled:

France	**Algeria, Tunisia, Madagascar, French Somaliland (Djibouti), French West Africa (Upper Volta [Burkina Faso], Ivory Coast, French Sudan [Mali], Mauritania, Niger, Senegal, Dahomey [Benin], French Guinea [Guinea]), Morocco, French Equatorial Africa (Gabon, Middle Congo [Democratic Republic of Congo], Oubangui-Chari [Central African Republic], Chad)**
Great Britain	**South Africa, Uganda, Kenya, Northern Rhodesia (Zambia), Southern Rhodesia (Zimbabwe), Egypt, Sudan, Nigeria, Gold Coast (Ghana), Nyasaland (Malawi), Bechuanaland (Botswana), Sierra Leone, Gambia, Anglo-Egyptian Sudan (Sudan), British Somaliland (Somalia), Basutoland (Lesotho), Swaziland, Zanzibar (Tanzania)**
Portugal	**Angola, Portuguese Guinea (Guinea-Bissau), Portuguese East Africa (Mozambique), the islands of Cape Verde, São Tomé, Príncipe, and Madeira**
Germany	**Tanganyika (Tanzania), Rwanda, Burundi, South West Africa (Namibia), Togoland (Togo), Kamerun (Cameroon)**
Belgium	**Congo (Democratic Republic of Congo)**
Italy	**Somaliland (Somalia), Eritrea, Libya**

Europeans wanted colonies that could supply raw materials for industries at home. There was a scramble for land. Each European country was afraid that the other countries would keep trade for themselves. African countries that would not sign trade agreements were taken by force. Many were tricked into signing agreements that they did not understand. By 1914, only Ethiopia and Liberia remained independent.

Some Africans resisted the invasion of their territory, but most were defeated. Peoples who at first accepted European rule became disillusioned. Many felt cheated and sought revenge, which often led to resistance and wars.

Africans tried to win back their freedom and some succeeded. Most, however, did not gain independence until the 1950s. European empires in Africa finally came to an end in the 1970s, when Portugal gave up large territories there and, in 1980, when Great Britain gave up colonial control of Zimbabwe.

Africa today

The Ashanti

The Ashanti lived in a tropical rain forest along the coast of the Gulf of Guinea in what is now called Ghana. They were farmers, hunters, and gatherers, and they mined gold. Many of these goods were traded with the people of the northern savanna country. Later, the Ashanti, like other nations, also became involved in slave trade. The desire to control this trade with the Europeans led to many conflicts among other African peoples.

In the late 1600s, **Osei Tutu**, a local Ashanti chief, convinced other clan chiefs to join in a military union. The chiefs agreed and together they defeated their rivals, the **Denkyira**. Tutu was then declared the leader of the newly formed Ashanti nation. The Ashanti Empire lasted for more than 200 years until the late 1880s, and was one of the larger empires in West Africa. In 1901, the British overran the government and made the Ashanti kingdom part of Great Britain's Gold Coast colony.

The African Slave Trade

The Portuguese first brought Africans to Europe as slaves in 1441. The Plague (see p. 76) had killed many Europeans, and there were not enough workers. The slaves were sold for high prices. Over the next sixty years, the Portuguese enslaved 50,000 Africans, mostly from West Africa.

When European countries established colonies in North, South, and Central America, the demand for slaves increased. European colonists did not want to do the heavy labor required to mine gold and silver or work the sugar plantations. Diseases from Europe had killed many of the Native Americans that the colonists had hoped would do the work. Some ten million Africans were sold as slaves in the Americas over 350 years. It is thought that at least one out of three Africans brought to America died either as a result of the journey or from bad treatment.

Africans were brought to the Americas on board crowded slave ships. Slaves were treated as cargo and tied down in the lower levels of the ship with little food and water and no privacy. As a result, many died on these ships and others became too ill to be sold at auction upon their arrival in the New World.

Chapter 5

Egyptians Rule Egypt

In 1805, **Muhammad Ali**, a Greek-born Turkish army officer, became ruler of Egypt. He expanded Egypt's power up the Nile by controlling the river. He built a strong army and conquered the Sudan. In addition, he wanted to make his country a modern state, and asked the Europeans for help. After his death, Egypt's rulers continued Ali's plans, but they were not as successful. The British soon took control of the Suez Canal, which linked the Mediterranean and Red seas. By 1882, the British had taken control of all Egypt.

In 1922, Egypt gained limited independence. The British agreed to leave the country by 1936 except the canal area, but World War II caused them to stay longer. Egyptians were tired of foreign control and wanted to be rid of it. Most Egyptians thought **King Farouk**, leader of the time, to be part of the problem. In 1952, the government was overthrown by a group of army officers led by **Gamal Abdel Nasser**. Nasser became the first Egyptian to rule Egypt after more than one thousand years of foreign control.

Gamal Abdel Nasser

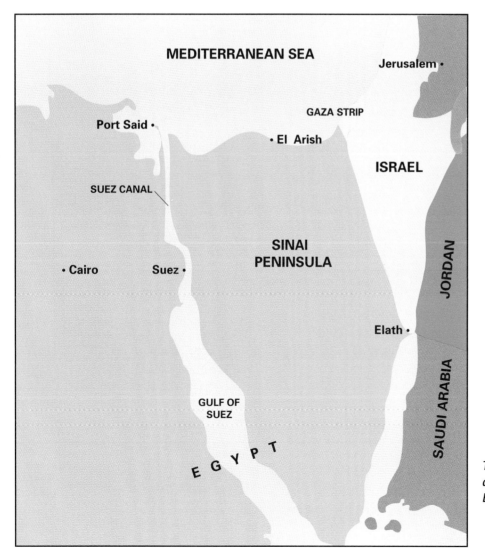

The 101-mile Suez Canal links the Mediterranean and Red seas and allows boats passage from Europe to Asia without navigating around Africa.

Chapter 6 South Africa

South Africa was originally inhabited by people called the **San**. They lived in the dry western part and hunted big game animals and gathered fruits and nuts. The San moved constantly, following food sources, and never built permanent homes.

Another people, called the **Khoikhoi**, lived near the San. They herded cattle and sheep as well as hunted and gathered. The San and the Khoikhoi are often referred to together as the **Khoisan**.

The eastern part of South Africa was occupied by groups of people who spoke Bantu languages. They farmed, raised livestock, and mined ore to make tools and weapons. The Bantu-speaking peoples made permanent homes and stayed in one place.

Bartolomeu Dias was a Portuguese sailor who sailed around the southern tip of Africa in 1488. He called it the Cape of Good Hope.

Around the mid-1600s, Dutch people began settling the southern tip of Africa. Their settlement was called Cape Colony. The Khoisan fought for their land, but were defeated and forced to work for the Dutch. More Europeans came and began to called themselves **Afrikaners**. The British called them **Boers**, which means "farmer" in Dutch. The mix of languages, particularly influenced by Dutch, was eventually called **Afrikaans**.

In the early nineteenth century, the British took Cape Colony from the Dutch. English became the main language and all slaves were freed. This angered the Afrikaner settlers, so they decided to search for new lands. Their migration became known as the **Great Trek** (journey).

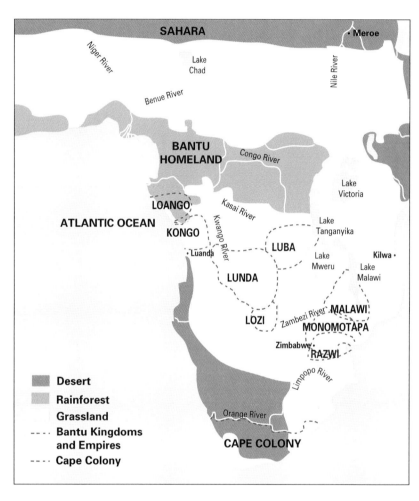

The Great Trek lasted for many years (1835–1840s) as the Afrikaners moved into the Bantu lands to the east and the north. They fought many battles, and most of the Bantu-speaking people lost their land. By 1854, the Afrikaners had won control and created two Afrikaner republics—the Transvaal and the Orange Free State. Slavery was abolished, but only white men could vote in these republics.

The British and the Afrikaners continued to fight over who should control the government, in part because of the discovery of diamond and gold mines in the area. In 1899, war broke out between the two and lasted until 1902. It was called the **South African War** (also called the **Boer War**) and ended with the British defeating the Afrikaners. The republics were joined and, in 1910, they formed the Union of South Africa. **Louis Botha**, a former Afrikaner general, became prime minister of an all-white government.

After the Europeans gave up control of Africa, the independence to much of Africa did not bring peace and prosperity to the new nations. Many countries were torn apart by civil wars, which resulted in military dictatorships. Few countries were ruled by civilian governments or elected their government officials. Rapid population growth and severe droughts caused hardships and famine (scarcity of food) in the 1980s.

In most countries, black majority rule came to power, some of which turned against the whites. In Zimbabwe in the 1990s, President Robert Mugabe began taking land away from whites without trials or compensation, resulting in much conflict and disregard for law.

In the early 1990s, an illness called acquired immune deficiency syndrome, commonly called **AIDS** (a disease that attacks the immune system), began to take a heavy toll on the entire population of Africa. This infectious (contagious) disease is the leading cause of death in southern Africa (countries located south of the Sahara Desert, also called sub-Saharan Africa). This portion of Africa makes up one-tenth of the world's population, but more than eighty percent of all AIDS deaths occur there. The AIDS epidemic is more severe there because most Africans cannot afford the medical drugs needed to combat the disease. The disease has left thousands of children orphaned and greatly reduced national life expectancy rates.

APARTHEID

South Africa became even more of a white man's land after the formation of the new union. The blacks living there were limited in many ways. The best jobs went to whites, and it was difficult for blacks to buy or rent land outside areas set aside for them. In 1948, the South African government made into law a policy called apartheid. This was a policy of separation by race—white, colored, Asian, or African (Bantu or other). Whites were defined as Europeans, coloreds as mixed races, Asians as people from India, and Bantu as black Africans.

Nelson Mandela

Apartheid forced people into white and nonwhite racial groups. This separation is called **segregation**. There were separate restaurants, restrooms, drinking fountains, and beaches. Marriage was banned between races, and whites and blacks had to live in separate areas. Often the areas designated for blacks to live in, called townships, were small and overcrowded. Much of the housing was nothing more than shacks with no electricity.

The **African National Congress (ANC)** was a group formed to protest the whites' unfair treatment of blacks. Protests became violent in the 1960s when white police shot into groups of blacks protesting in the streets.

One of the leaders of the ANC was **Nelson Mandela**. He fought for a democratic and free society in which all people are equal. In 1962, he was arrested and charged with attempting to overthrow the government. An all-white jury found him guilty. Mandela served twenty-seven years in jail and was released in 1990 by **F. W. De Klerk**, president of South Africa. De Klerk and Mandela worked together to run the government. In 1993, both Mandela and De Klerk won the Nobel Peace Prize for their efforts. In 1994, Mandela was elected president of South Africa.

Chapter 1 Mesoamerica

The first advanced civilizations in the western hemisphere originated in the area called **Mesoamerica**, the region that is now Mexico and Central America, and around the western coast of South America. In these areas, several advanced civilizations developed, similar to those found in other parts of the world. Their chief crop was corn. Textiles, pottery, and jewelry of gold and silver were produced. There were city centers with canals and gardens, temples, and pyramids. Priest-emperors ruled and built armies, courts, and schools. Little is known about them because many of their written records were destroyed before their language could be understood by Europeans.

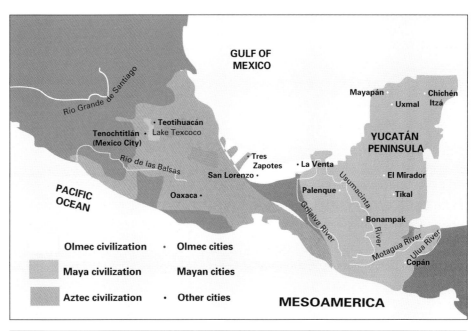

Major Peoples of Mesoamerica

Aztec	Maya	Olmec	Teotihuacán	Totonac
Coahuiltecan	Mixtec	Tarascan	Toltec	Zapotec

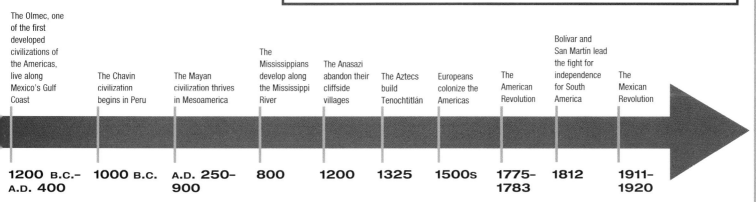

The Olmec, one of the first developed civilizations of the Americas, live along Mexico's Gulf Coast	The Chavin civilization begins in Peru	The Mayan civilization thrives in Mesoamerica	The Mississippians develop along the Mississippi River	The Anasazi abandon their cliffside villages	The Aztecs build Tenochtitlán	Europeans colonize the Americas	The American Revolution	Bolívar and San Martín lead the fight for independence for South America	The Mexican Revolution
1200 B.C.–A.D. 400	1000 B.C.	A.D. 250–900	800	1200	1325	1500s	1775–1783	1812	1911–1920

55

The Olmec

One of the first developed civilizations was that of the Olmec. They lived along Mexico's Gulf Coast between 1200 and 400 B.C. They were farmers and lived in thatched huts. The Olmec were a religious people ruled by priests. They built large temples, monuments, and pyramids to glorify their leaders. The Olmec are known for their great carved heads of stone, thought to be of Olmec rulers. More than sixteen have been uncovered.

The Olmec developed the first calendar in the Americas. They also developed a counting system. Because of these and other achievements in art and politics, the Olmec were a great influence on later civilizations.

The Olmec civilization flourished for about 800 years, then disappeared.

The Maya

The Maya built one of the most highly developed civilizations of Mesoamerica. They flourished between A.D. 250 and 900 in and around the Yucatán Peninsula (present-day southern Mexico, Belize, Guatemala, Honduras, and western El Salvador).

Most of the Maya were farmers who grew corn, squash, and cotton. They built at least eighty cities for trade, the largest of which was Tikal. The Maya were ruled by a noble class. Only people in this class could serve in the government or become priests. The king was the chief ruler and thought to have godlike qualities. Priests conducted the religious ceremonies. They were held in high regard because every part of Mayan life had some kind of religious connection.

The Maya developed a system of writing and a calendar and were skilled in mathematics and astronomy. They built extraordinary monuments and buildings, some of which they decorated with wall paintings.

Cobata is the largest of the Olmec carved heads, standing eleven feet high; it was carved between 1200 and 900 B.C.

Mayan Gods

Itzamná	The god of creation. The name means "lizard house."
Ixchel	Moon goddess, patroness of weaving, medicine, and childbirth.
Kukulcán	A feathered serpent considered to be the god of kings.

ACCOMPLISHMENTS OF THE MAYA

1 They developed two calendars and a way to calculate time. The solar calendar had 365 days and was used for seasonal planting. The other was a 260-day festival calendar used for religious ceremonies.

2 They developed a mathematical system that included zero.

3 They developed a good knowledge of astronomy through careful observation of the sun, moon, stars, and planets.

4 They developed a writing system of symbols, or glyphs, the most complex in America.

5 They built 200-foot-high pyramids and elaborate temples, made pottery, and carved ornaments from jade.

The Aztecs

The Aztecs originally settled on Lake Texcoco in the early 1200s. After 200 years of constant warring, they conquered all the neighboring peoples. By the time the Spanish arrived in the 1500s, the Aztecs ruled a mighty empire in central and southern Mexico.

The capital of the Aztec Empire and the center of Aztec life was the city of Tenochtitlán (near modern Mexico City). The engineering skills of the Aztecs provided roads, raised channels to carry fresh water, and constructed dikes for irrigating the gardens throughout the city. Tlatelolco, the large marketplace in the capital, was a crossroads for trade where people came from all over to exchange goods.

The Aztec society was highly organized. There was one ruler, or emperor. Nobles ruled cities and served as judges. Priests performed religious duties, and the common people made up the majority of the population.

Religion was very important to the Aztecs. Magnificent temples and pyramids were built to honor the gods. The chief god was ***Huitzilopochtli***, the god of sun and war. The Aztecs believed he needed regular human sacrifices in order to remain strong. Prisoners and slaves were used as victims, but sometimes the Aztecs' own people were chosen. To be sacrificed was an honor and believed to grant eternal life.

The Main Aztec Gods

Huitzilopochtli   God of war and god of the sun.

Tezcatlipoca   The most powerful god, associated with destiny or fate.

Quetzalcóatl   The feathered serpent, god of learning and priesthood.

Elaborate headdresses were worn in Aztec ceremonies. The Aztec allowed only royalty or the nobility to use the tail plumes of the quetzal bird.

The Spanish Conquer the Aztecs

In 1519, a Spaniard named **Hernán Cortés** (see p. 66) and 500 soldiers marched into Tenochtitlán looking for gold. The Aztec emperor **Montezuma** gave them gold and other gifts. The Spanish took Montezuma prisoner and overtook the city with their guns, horses, and cannons—things the Aztecs had never seen before. There were numerous battles between the Aztecs and the Spanish. Many of the conquered people sided with the Spanish and the Spanish won. The Spaniards destroyed a great deal of the city to put up their own buildings. The new city was called Mexico City.

The Andean Civilizations

Another civilization developed along the western coast of South America in present-day Peru. These people lived in and around the Andes Mountains.

THE CHAVIN

The Chavin were one of the earliest cultures to develop in South America. They lived in northern Peru from about 1000 to 200 B.C. At Chavin de Huantar, the center of their culture, the Chavin built a magnificent temple. The Chavin developed excellent stone carvings and fine pottery and ceramics. Some of the oldest gold work has been found among their ruins.

THE MOCHE

The Moche civilization developed along the Moche River in northern Peru from about A.D. 200 to 800. Its people built grand pyramids, including the **Temple of the Sun**, a terraced pyramid made entirely of **adobe** bricks (adobe is a mixture of mud and straw that is baked hard by the sun). During an archaeological dig in 1987, the tombs of Moche rulers were discovered, filled with gold and copper ornaments set with jewels. It proved that the Moche were among the greatest artisans of the ancient world.

THE INCAS

The Inca Empire is the most famous of the Andean civilizations. The Inca Empire began to develop about the same time as the Aztec Empire and was at its most powerful in the late fifteenth century. It was the largest empire of its time, stretching about 3,000 miles along the coast of South America in the Andes Mountains. Its population was about six million people. (England had about four million people at the same time.) The capital was Cuzco.

THE RISE AND FALL OF THE INCA EMPIRE

Two great rulers expanded the Inca Empire. **Pachacutec**, the ninth Inca emperor, was the first. **Topa**, his son, was the second. The Inca were at their most powerful during the reigns of those leaders, from 1438 to 1493. They united the people of the Andean region to form one great empire by forcing their government, law, religion, and language on the people they conquered.

After Topa died, the government became weak and civil wars began to break out. At about this time, **Francisco Pizarro** and his Spanish soldiers invaded the empire. They took the ruler, **Atahualpa**, prisoner and killed him. The Spanish took over the Inca Empire, and it became part of the Spanish Empire.

ACCOMPLISHMENTS OF THE INCAS

1 They developed the Quechua language (but no real system of writing).

2 They developed a method of counting and keeping records using quipu, a process of tying knots in strings. Using this method, they took a census and collected taxes.

3 They were highly skilled builders who cut stones by hand and built without the use of mortar. The stones were placed so tightly that many buildings are still standing today. They also built a great network of stone roads, covering more than 15,000 miles.

4 They produced many beautiful works of art, including weavings and skilled metal workings.

Built by the Incas, Machu Picchu covers an area of five square miles and was built on a series of terraces carved into the side of a mountain more than 7,000 feet above sea level. The origins are unknown, but it is thought to have been a summer residence of emperors.

Chapter 2 North America

Native Americans lived in North America as early as 9000 B.C. Many lived in southeastern Canada and east of the Mississippi in the United States. They hunted the deciduous forests and gathered roots and berries in the open country. Native Americans that settled in the West were also hunters.

The Adena

An advanced group of Native Americans lived in southern Ohio, Indiana, Kentucky, and West Virginia. They were called the Adena and they thrived about 1000 B.C. They built large mounds of earth to cover the tombs of their rulers. Their people raised corn, squash, and beans. The Adena were also skilled at making pottery.

These **Mound Builders** were skilled at farming and crafts and influenced the **Hopewell** people, who flourished mostly in southern Ohio and the Mississippi River valleys from about 200 B.C. to A.D. 400. The Hopewell centers were in present-day Illinois, with smaller centers in Kansas City and other places along the Mississippi River. The Hopewell were also Mound Builders. Their mounds were large and rectangular, while others were in the shape of animals. These mounds were possibly religious, ceremonial, and burial centers.

About A.D. 800, another culture, the **Mississippian**, developed. The Mississippians lived along the Mississippi River near present-day St. Louis, Missouri. Their capital was called **Cahokia** and lay at the junction of the Missouri and Mississippi rivers. The Mississippians were also Mound Builders, and they built a large earth mound platform, about 1,000 feet long and 700 feet wide, in the center of Cahokia. Temples, plazas, and other conical mounds were built around it.

Cahokia was a center for trade along the two rivers. The Mississippians traded food products, leather goods, and pottery with other peoples, both north and south of them. The Mississippian culture was spread throughout the eastern woodlands. The Mississippians were the ancestors of many later Native Americans, such as the Creek, Choctaw, Chickasaw, and many others.

Cahokia had been abandoned by the time the Europeans arrived in the Americas.

The Anasazi

About the same time that the Hopewell culture was developing in the eastern United States, the Anasazi culture was developing in the Southwest. The Anasazi were a highly skilled people who lived and prospered on very dry land in what is today New Mexico, Arizona, Utah, and Colorado. There was little rain, and in order to grow crops, the Anasazi created an irrigation system of canals. These canals ran to the fields. During the rainy season, the streams would overflow into the canals and water the fields.

The Anasazi built large villages of adobe on the sides of cliffs. These villages were like large apartment houses. Many were several stories high and one had more than 800 rooms.

The Anasazi left their villages around 1300 partly because of a long drought. The ruins can still be seen today in the Southwest.

The Anasazi are the ancestors of today's Pueblo, which include the Hopi, Zuni, and Acoma.

Pueblos — large adobe "apartment buildings" — were built on cliffsides by the Pueblo peoples known as the Anasazi.

Chapter 3 uropeans Coloniz the Americas

Spain, France, and Great Britain all sent explorers to the Americas. Later, they established colonies, which were settled by people seeking freedom, wealth, or adventure. The European governments hoped that the colonies would send them valuable minerals (such as gold and silver), furs, and agricultural products (such as tobacco, lumber, potatoes, indigo, and fur). The colonies provided the European countries with markets for both manufactured goods and slaves.

French explorers claimed the land from Canada to the Great Lakes, and down the Mississippi River to the Gulf of Mexico. They called this territory **New France.** By 1750, almost 100,000 French fur traders and missionaries lived there. Unlike the English, the French did not establish large settlements. Instead, they set up trading posts, and some even lived off the land like the Native Americans. Britain controlled thirteen colonies along the Atlantic coast of North America. Spain claimed Florida, establishing a fort at St. Augustine. It also claimed most of what is today Texas, New Mexico, Arizona, and California, as well as present-day Mexico, where it had conquered the Aztec Empire.

By the 1500s, Spain and Portugal had control of Central and South America.

The 13 Original Colonies of the United States of America

New England colonies	Middle colonies	Southern colonies
Connecticut	Delaware	Georgia
Massachusetts	Maryland	North Carolina
New Hampshire	New Jersey	South Carolina
Rhode Island	New York	Virginia
	Pennsylvania	

63

The American Revolution (1775–1783)

By 1775, there were serious tensions between the thirteen British colonies in North America and the mother country, Great Britain. Among other reasons, the colonists felt they were being taxed too heavily and unfairly because they were not represented in the British Parliament. The British thought it only fair that the colonies should help pay for their defense. Many colonists called for independence from Great Britain. In 1781, the thirteen colonies won their revolution against the British, and the United States of America was born.

minuteman

redcoat

Minutemen were members of groups of armed men who were ready in a minute's notice to take to the field against the British. British troops were nicknamed "redcoats" because of the color of their jackets. In 1768, the city of Boston was occupied by British soldiers. On March 5, 1770, a number of colonists got in an argument with the redcoats and began throwing snowballs and chunks of ice at them. The soldiers fired shots into the angry but unarmed crowd. Five Americans were killed. Sam Adams called this event the Boston Massacre. The British soldiers were brought to court. Sam Adams's cousin, John Adams, defended the soldiers. Two were found guilty of manslaughter and the others were declared innocent. Revolutionaries publicized this story to build support for colonial independence.

RESULTS OF THE REVOLUTIONARY WAR

1 The thirteen colonies became the independent United States of America and were recognized by Great Britain.

2 Britain gave the United States the land east of the Mississippi River, north to Canada, and south to the border of Florida.

3 All British trade restrictions were lifted.

4 A new government with elected representatives was formed under the Articles of Confederation.

5 The successful revolution encouraged other people, especially the French, to overthrow their own governments.

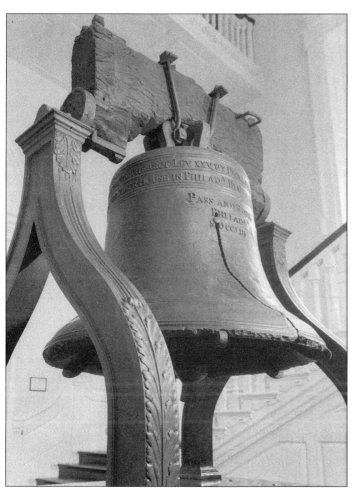

There have been two Liberty Bells. The first one was made in London and arrived in Philadelphia in 1752. The bell cracked when it was tested. The second bell was made in Philadelphia. It cracked sometime between 1817 and 1846. Bolts were inserted in an effort to keep the bell from cracking further.

The Liberty Bell, which hangs in Liberty Bell Center near Independence Hall in Philadelphia, Pennsylvania, bears an inscription from Leviticus 25:10: "Proclaim liberty throughout all the land unto all the inhabitants thereof."

Chapter 4

Mexico

By 1540, within twenty-five years after **Hernán Cortés** destroyed Tenochtitlán, the capital city of the Aztecs (see p. 58), Spanish explorers claimed land from California to Texas, all along the Gulf coast to Florida, and south to Panama. This entire colony was called **New Spain**.

The people of New Spain were divided into four main groups: Those who had been born in Spain and ruled the colony were called **peninsulares**. The **criollos**, or Creoles, were the children of Spaniards born in New Spain. They often owned large ranches and farms, but were not allowed to hold high government posts. The **mestizos**, of Spanish and Indian ancestry, worked as farmers, craftspeople, and laborers. The **native Indians** were forced to work on large farms or in the gold and silver mines.

Mexico was ruled by the Spanish as New Spain for 300 years until the Creoles acted upon their resentment of the peninsulares, who ruled Mexico.

Mexican Independence

In 1810, a Creole priest named **Miguel Hidalgo y Costilla**, from the village of Dolores, led a revolt of Mexican Indians and mestizos to Mexico City. Although he was defeated and executed, it was the beginning of the struggle for independence. Ten years later, another revolt, led by **Agustín de Iturbide**, finally broke Spanish rule. Iturbide crowned himself Emperor Agustín I, but his rule did not last. A new congress elected General **Guadalupe Victoria** as the first president of the federal republic in 1824.

After a war with the United States from 1846 to 1848, Mexico lost all of its territory north of the Rio Grande River. In 1862, France invaded Mexico. One of Mexico's greatest leaders, a Zapotec Indian named **Benito Juárez**, led the fight to drive out the French. He crushed the regime of the French-installed emperor, the Hapsburg Archduke Maximilian, the brother of the Austrian emperor **Franz Josef I**. As president of Mexico, Juárez tried to rebuild the country, constructing roads and railroads and supporting free education.

The Mexican Revolution

In 1876, **Porfirio Díaz** took over Mexico, first as president and later as dictator. A mestizo, Díaz ruled, with a short break, for thirty-four years. He restored order and progress, encouraging foreign investment and industry. Despite this progress, Mexican Indians and other poor people were denied liberty and land.

By 1910, resentment against Díaz was becoming widespread. **Francisco Madero**, a wealthy Creole, wanted to help the poor. He wrote a book about political freedom and traveled around the country telling people about it. When he became popular, Díaz put him in jail. Upon his release, Madero was supported by **Pancho Villa**, a former bandit, in a revolt against Díaz. Díaz fled the country in 1911. Emiliano Zapata (see box below) led rebels in the south. Zapata's men led raids against the rich and turned over the **haciendas**, or large estates, to the poor.

A new constitution was written in 1917, and the revolution officially ended in the 1920s. In 1934, General **Lázaro Cárdenas** became president. He supported the working class and reformed the land distribution laws, granted freedom of speech, and took over the foreign-owned oil industry.

Heroes of the Mexican Revolution

Two of the most famous heroes of the Mexican Revolution were **Pancho Villa** and **Emiliano Zapata**. Villa led raids in the north, and Zapata in the south.

Pancho Villa had once been an outlaw. He put together an army of bandits and peasants. They robbed the rich, stole cattle, and fought the **federales**, government soldiers. Villa had an unusual hit-and-run style of fighting that made him very popular with the Mexican people. A large man with a roaring laugh, he rode a black horse called Lucifer and twirled his pistols in the air. He always tricked the federales and disappeared into the wilderness.

Pancho Villa

Emiliano Zapata was a rebel leader in the south. He banded together an army of peasants. These workers were loyal to Zapata because he believed the land belonged to them. He rode a great white horse and his battle cry was "land and liberty." He and his men raided large sugar plantations and gave the land back to the peasants who originally farmed it. Zapata's ideas of land reform later became part of the constitution. Both Villa and Zapata were killed and became legends in history and song.

Thousands of women, called **soldaderas**, also joined the revolution. They fought bravely alongside the men. A famous soldadera was Adelita. A song was written about her bravery and is still sung today in Mexico.

Emiliano Zapata

Chapter 5

Canada

In 1497, **John Cabot**, a Venetian explorer for England, was the first European since the Vikings to reach Canada. In 1608, a French explorer named **Samuel de Champlain** sailed to Canada and founded the colony of Quebec on the St. Lawrence River. Some years later, in 1670, the English came to Canada and established the **Hudson's Bay Company**. This eventually led to a war between England and France.

In 1754, competition for land and the profitable fur trade led to the French and Indian War. England defeated France, which lost nearly all of its holdings in North America. England then took control of Canada.

During the American Revolution, the Canadians remained loyal to England. There were two reasons for this: fear of the power of the United States and differences in religion. Almost all French Canadians were Roman Catholic and the United States was mostly Protestant.

Canadian Independence

In 1791, the British divided Canada into Upper Canada and Lower Canada. Lower Canada was French-speaking Quebec and Upper Canada was the English-speaking majority. In 1837, the Canadians revolted against the British. The revolt was a failure. However, England recognized that a revolution would happen sooner or later and allowed the colony to elect its own government. Finally, with the British North America Act of 1867, Canada became the Dominion of Canada. This gave Canada almost full control over its own affairs. It had self-rule, but a governor-general was appointed by the British crown. It was not until 1982 that Canada became totally independent of Britain. At that time, Canadians wrote their own constitution.

The Provinces of Canada

Alberta

British Columbia

Manitoba

New Brunswick

Newfoundland and Labrador

Nova Scotia

Ontario

Prince Edward Island

Saskatchewan

Quebec

A maple leaf, the symbol of Canada, appears on the national flag.

Canada also has three territories—Yukon Territory, Northwest Territories, and Nunavut.

The four original provinces were Ontario, Quebec, Nova Scotia, and New Brunswick.

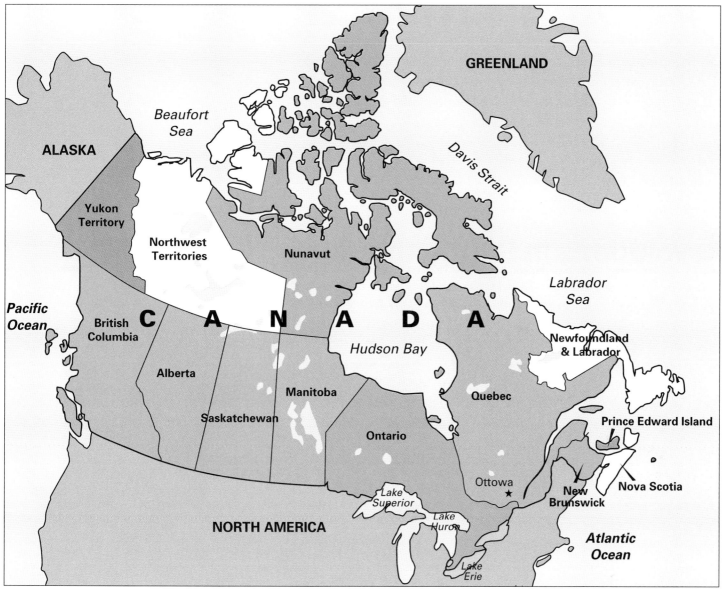

Canadian Provinces

Chapter 6

Central and South America

Europeans first arrived in Central and South America in the late 1400s. By the 1500s, nearly all of these lands were controlled by Spain and Portugal. Spurred by the revolutions in other parts of the Western Hemisphere such as the American Revolution in 1776 and Haiti's revolt against the French, which ended in independence for Haiti in 1804, South America began to demand freedom. By the mid-1800s, most countries were independent.

Revolutions in South America

In the early 1800s, a series of rebellions started from Mexico in the north to Argentina in the south. In the south, **José de San Martín** led the fight for independence in Argentina and Peru. **Bernardo O'Higgins** defeated the Spanish in Chile.

In the north, the leader of the fight against Spain was **Simón Bolívar**. Bolívar was a wealthy Venezuelan general. When he was young, he traveled to Europe and was influenced by the ideas of freedom springing up there. Upon his return, he dedicated the rest of his life toward working to liberate Spain's colonies. Starting in 1810, Bolívar fought many battles in Venezuela and in the colony of New Granada, which is today Colombia. One of his major victories was in the Battle of Boyacá in Colombia in 1819. This victory was a turning point in Colombia's struggle for independence.

Bolívar combined his armies with those of San Martín in Peru and Ecuador, captured port cities, and declared the independence of Peru in 1821. However, it was not until 1824 that all of the Spanish were driven out of Peru. Peru and many of the countries were liberated (freed) from Spanish rule around 1830. A new country, formerly part of Peru, was named Bolivia for Bolívar, the great leader of Spanish independence.

Simón Bolívar

Brazilian Independence

The Portuguese royal family left Portugal in 1807 when Napoleon I threatened their country. They went to Brazil and this became the new center of the Portuguese Empire. King **John VI** ruled until 1821, when he had to return home. His son, **Dom Pedro**, became ruler. The parliament tried to undo King John's reforms and denounced Portugal. Dom Pedro agreed with the Brazilians and refused to return to Portugal. On September 7, 1822, Dom Pedro declared Brazil an independent country. Brazil had won its freedom with very little bloodshed.

South America, about 1822

MEXICO
Gulf of Mexico
Caribbean Sea
Belize
Honduras
★ Mexico City
Nicaragua
Guatemala
Cartagena •
★ Caracas
GUYANA
SURINAME
San Salvador
Costa Rica
• Tunja
VENEZUELA
1830
FRENCH GUIANA
Panama
★ Bogotá
COLOMBIA
1819
★ Quito
ECUADOR
1819
PERU
1821
BRAZIL
1822
★ Lima
• Cuzco
BOLIVIA
1825
★ La Paz
Pacific
Ocean
CHILE
1818
PARAGUAY
1811
ANDES MOUNTAINS
Atlantic
Ocean
URUGUAY
1828
ARGENTINA
1816

- - - - - **Country borderlines**
- **Formerly controlled by Spain**
- **Formerly controlled by Portugal**
- **Formerly controlled by France**
- **Formerly controlled by England**
- **Formerly controlled by Holland**

(Dates indicate year of liberation from Spanish or Portuguese rule)

Europe (A.D. 800–1800)

The Making of Modern Europe

The era of European history from about A.D. 500 to 1500 is known as the Middle Ages, or the **medieval period**, because the word *medieval* is Latin for "of the middle ages." The era began at the end of the Roman Empire and continued until the modern nations of France and England were established.

Charlemagne's Medieval Empire

Charlemagne was the outstanding ruler in medieval Europe for 46 years, from 768 to 814. A great warrior who extended his kingdom over most of western Europe by 800, Charlemagne controlled the largest expanse in Europe since the Roman Empire. His aim was not just to rule but to spread Christianity. **Pope Leo III** was so thankful that he crowned Charlemagne the **Holy Roman Emperor**; his empire would be called the **Holy Roman Empire**.

During his reign, Charlemagne's empire became the most orderly and unified in Europe. He set up a central government and divided his vast holdings into provinces ruled by nobles who reported to him. He built impressive monuments, theaters, and a forum. Charlemagne placed great importance on education and established schools all over his empire.

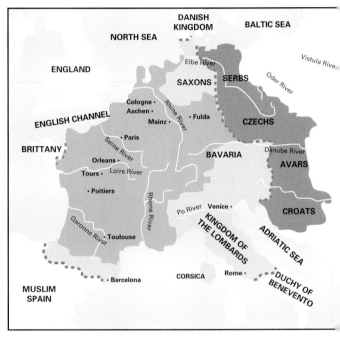

Holy Roman Empire, about 800. In green is the territory Charlemagne took over in 768. In dark yellow is the territory he conquered and made part of his empire. In purple is the territory where people paid taxes to Charlemagne but governed themselves.

Charlemagne is crowned Holy Roman Emperor by Pope Leo III	The Crusades between European Christians and Muslim Turks for control of the Holy Land are fought	The Renaissance begins	The Plague, or Black Death, begins in Europe	Martin Luther starts the Reformation by calling for reform in the church	The Romanov family takes control of Russia and rules for 300 years	The French Revolution starts	Napoleon Bonaparte takes control of France
A.D. 800	1095–1291	1300	1347	1517	1613	1789	1799

The Feudal System

Feudalism was a system of government and a way of life that restored order in Europe after the fall of Rome. At that time, there were no formal countries but hundreds of **fiefdoms**. People who were given land were expected to be loyal to the landowner. In return, they were protected against invaders. There were three classes of people during that time: The **nobles** were the kings and lords; priests, bishops, and cardinals were called the **clergy**; and the **peasants** worked as farmers, builders, and craftspeople.

Under the feudal system, nobles (also called lords) gave land and protection to **vassals**, or lesser lords, who usually paid taxes to a lord and provided him with military service. The land the vassal received was called a **manor**. Many of the peasants who worked on the manors were **serfs**. Serfs were not slaves but could not leave the manor unless the lord permitted it. Most of the work done on a noble's large estate was done by serfs.

The lords and ladies lived in castles on the estates. Young nobles in training were called **squires**. Once a squire had learned the skills and duties of a nobleman, he became a soldier for the lord. These soldiers were called **knights**.

William the Conqueror

In 1066, England was invaded by the Normans from France at the Battle of Hastings. William, Duke of Normandy, wanted to defeat the English king **Harold**. After a long battle, Harold was killed and William succeeded him, becoming known as **William the Conqueror**. He was crowned on Christmas Day, 1066. William established a stable government and was responsible for the start of feudalism in England.

The Age of Faith

The Middle Ages is often called the Age of Faith because the church in Rome was more powerful than any government. Most people in Europe were Christians, and religion was the center of life and learning.

Many people dedicated their lives to service in the church. Men became priests and women became nuns. Some became **monks**, religious men who lived in groups outside of society in the countryside or desert. **St. Benedict of Nursia** was one of the most well-known monks. He started a **monastery** (a place where monks live), and his order, or group, became known as the Benedictines. The Benedictines built schools, churches, and libraries, and fed the poor. Their organization grew throughout the world by stressing the need to serve others.

Eventually, the Christian church divided. For many years, differences had been developing between the eastern and western halves of the church. One of the main differences between the two was over who should head the church. In the East, the Byzantine emperor ruled both church and state. In the West, the pope ruled the church while kings and queens ruled the various countries. Finally, in 1054, the two churches split. In the East, the Christian church became known as the **Eastern Orthodox Church**. In the West, it became known as the **Roman Catholic Church**.

The Crusades

The Crusades were a series of religious wars that took place from 1095 to 1291. The purpose of the Crusades was for the European Christians to defeat the Muslim Turks for control of the Holy Land—that part of the Middle East where Jesus had lived, especially the city of Jerusalem. It had been taken by the Seljuk Turks in 1085. When the Seljuks next planned to invade Constantinople, the Byzantines asked for help. Pope Urban II organized the Crusades to recapture the Holy Land, but, even after almost 200 years and several major Crusades, the Christians still did not succeed.

SIGNIFICANT EARLY CRUSADES

1 The First Crusade (1095–1099). It took the first army of European knights two years to reach Turkey, where they defeated the Turkish army, despite being outnumbered. Later, the knights captured Jerusalem. The Crusaders set up small kingdoms around the cities of Jerusalem, Edessa, Antioch, and Tripoli.

2 The Second Crusade (1147–1149). The Seljuk Turks recaptured the city of Edessa in 1144. This started a new Crusade that began several years later in 1147 and was joined by King Louis VII and his wife, Queen Eleanor of Aquitaine of France (see box).

3 The Third Crusade (1189–1192). The Third Crusade was caused by the capture of Jerusalem by the Muslim leader Saladin in 1187. This Crusade was led by three kings: Frederick I of Germany, Philip II of France, and Richard I of England (Richard the Lion-Hearted). The Third Crusade ended when Richard and Saladin agreed to make peace for five years.

Crusaders were the knights of Europe. They dressed in the armor and chain mail typical of medieval European times.

Eleanor of Aquitaine and Richard the Lion-Hearted

Eleanor of Aquitaine was one of the first women to challenge the church and her two husbands for equality. Eleanor was born wealthy and had a good education. Her father, ***Duke William of Aquitaine***, raised her to rule his land in central and southwestern France. When he died, many men wanted to marry her for control of the land. She married ***Louis VII*** of France and became queen of France. But Louis would not allow her to rule equally with him despite the fact that she had brought more territory to the kingdom than he had, so Eleanor had the church dissolve her marriage. She then married King ***Henry II*** of England and had five sons and three daughters, but Henry would not share power with her either.

　　Richard I (the Lion-Hearted) was the favorite son of Eleanor. He and two of his brothers had plotted to overthrow their father, Henry II, in 1173. The plan failed, and their father forgave them, so that in 1189, Richard became king of England. He was very popular, but spent much of his ten-year reign fighting in the Crusades. He received the name Richard the Lion-Hearted because he was such a brave and able knight. Legend has it that Richard was so well liked that even his enemy, ***Saladin*** of Constantinople, said that if he were to lose Jerusalem, he would rather lose it to Richard than to anyone else. During Richard's time away at the Crusades, Eleanor ruled in his place. She governed well, was just, and established some rights for women.

The Magna Carta

King John was crowned king of England in 1199 after the death of Richard I. After increasing taxes and having a long feud with the pope, nobles and clergy forced King John to sign the ***Magna Carta***, which means "great charter." The Magna Carta strongly limited the power of the king.

MAJOR POINTS OF THE MAGNA CARTA

- **The king is the absolute ruler but he has to obey the laws.**
- **The king cannot limit the freedom of the church.**
- **The king cannot tax land without a meeting of the Great Council, the leading twenty-five landowners.**
- **The king cannot put any free person in jail without a trial.**

The Hundred Years' War (1337–1453)

The Norman kings of England were the feudal lords over large sections of French territory. The French rulers wanted to reign over their land. The French became angry when King ***Edward III*** of England claimed to also be king of France. The French invaded English-held territory and an on-again, off-again war began between England and France; it lasted for over a hundred years. This struggle became known as the Hundred Years' War.

The Hundred Years' War did not end until 1453, when the French drove the English from the city of Bordeaux, France. England would no longer be a power on the continent of Europe.

France, about 1400

75

Joan of Arc

A young girl named **Joan of Arc**, from the French region of Lorraine, led several major battles during the Hundred Years' War. She was only sixteen when she convinced Prince Charles of France, later King **Charles VII**, to let her build an army. Joan's clear, direct leadership inspired enthusiasm and resulted in many victories, including the important **Battle of Orléans**. Joan became a heroine, but she was later captured by the English, sentenced to death by a church court for witchcraft and heresy, and burned at the stake. Centuries later, the Catholic church named her a saint.

Joan of Arc

The Black Death

In 1347, an Italian ship returned from the east to Messina, Italy. Sailors came ashore bringing with them a terrible disease known as the **Plague**, or Black Death. It spread quickly across Europe because people knew little about medicine or the need to be clean. Many thought the Plague was caused by God's anger. About one person in every three died from the Plague between 1347 and 1351. In Paris alone, it is estimated that 50,000 people died.

It was hundreds of years before anyone discovered the cause of the Black Death. It was a germ that came from fleas that lived on rats. The rats could have been controlled by cats, but at that time cats had been slaughtered in great numbers because some people believed they were the agents of the devil.

The Renaissance

The Renaissance was a European revival of learning and the arts that began about 1300 in northern Italy. The Renaissance reached its peak in the early 1500s in Rome. It gradually spread throughout northern Europe. Wealthy families became **patrons**, or supporters of the arts, paying for works of art, libraries, books, and buildings. The leading Renaissance patrons were the popes in Rome, the **Medici** family in Florence, the **Sforza** family in Milan, and wealthy merchants in Venice.

The Renaissance produced great artists like **Michelangelo** and **Leonardo da Vinci**. It also was a period of scientific progress and exploration of the world beyond Europe.

DIFFERENCES BETWEEN THE RENAISSANCE AND THE AGE OF FAITH

1 The Renaissance celebrated the individual, rather than the group.

2 Interest in the ideas of ancient Greece and Rome returned during the Renaissance.

3 People enjoyed worldly pleasure and rejected the simple lifestyle of feudal times during the Renaissance.

HIGHLIGHTS OF RENAISSANCE ACHIEVEMENTS

ART

Sandro Botticelli. An Italian, known for realistic paintings such as *Venus and Mars* and *The Birth of Venus*, this artist celebrated the classical culture of Greece and Rome.

Michelangelo Buonarroti. An Italian painter, sculptor, poet, and architect, he painted the Sistine Chapel in the Basilica of St. Peter's in the Vatican, carved the sculptures of *David* and the *Pietà* (which is a statue of Mary and Jesus), and designed the dome of St. Peter's.

Leonardo da Vinci. An Italian painter, sculptor, architect, musician, engineer, and scientist, he was considered a genius. Two of his most famous paintings are *Mona Lisa* and *The Last Supper*, which shows Jesus with his disciples.

Raphael (Raffaello Santi). An Italian who painted many religious works such as the *Sistine Madonna* (Mary, the Mother of Jesus) as well as many other paintings in St. Peter's.

Rembrandt van Rijn. Often considered the greatest painter of northern Europe, he was known for portraits of common people. He was from the Netherlands.

LITERATURE

Dante Alighieri. The first to write an important book in Italian, rather than Latin, Dante is best known for *The Divine Comedy*, a long poem considered a literary masterpiece.

Miguel de Cervantes. A Spanish writer whose masterpiece, *Don Quixote*, poked fun at knighthood and feudal society.

Geoffrey Chaucer. The author of *The Canterbury Tales*, a collection of stories about traveling pilgrims on their way to the religious shrine in Canterbury, England.

Niccolò Machiavelli. An Italian who wrote a book called *The Prince*, which was a guide book for political rulers on how to gain and maintain power.

William Shakespeare. Considered the greatest English poet and playwright, he wrote many plays, such as *Romeo and Juliet*, *Julius Caesar*, and *Macbeth*.

SCIENCE AND TECHNOLOGY

Nicolaus Copernicus. An astronomer who observed that the sun, not Earth, is the center of the universe, contrary to what the church taught people to believe.

René Descartes. A philosopher and mathematician, was the founder of modern geometry.

Galileo Galilei. An astronomer, mathematician, and philosopher who improved the telescope and confirmed Copernicus's theory that the planets revolve around the sun.

Johannes Gutenberg. Inventor of the printing press, about 1450, making it possible to print books cheaply and quickly. Prior to this, books were copied by hand.

William Harvey. A doctor who demonstrated that blood circulates throughout the body.

Gutenberg printing press

The Reformation

The Protestant Reformation was a religious revolt, or protest, against the Roman Catholic Church. A German clergyman, **Martin Luther**, was the person responsible for starting the movement in 1517.

The church had grown very rich and powerful and nearly all Europeans were Catholic. However, some people questioned the church's authority when it began the practice of selling *indulgences*, or pardons, for sin. Believing you shouldn't have to buy your way into heaven, Martin Luther became angry. Luther believed that to gain heaven all you needed was to have faith in God as told in the New Testament. The problem was that most people couldn't read the Bible because it was written in Latin. Luther listed this complaint and others on a statement called the **Ninety-five Theses**. He nailed this statement to the door of the church in Wittenberg, Germany. His writings were printed and distributed and his teachings began to spread over Europe.

In 1521, Pope **Leo X** excommunicated (banned) Luther from the Catholic church, and Holy Roman Emperor **Charles V** declared him an outlaw. While in hiding, he translated the Bible into German so people could read and understand it. Eventually, people left the Catholic church to form their own churches. People who believed Luther's teachings were called **Lutherans**.

Other Protestant movements began all over Europe. In Switzerland, **John Calvin** believed that God had already chosen a group, the elect, for heaven. This group became known as Calvinists, and were the origin of today's Presbyterians. In England, King **Henry VIII** wanted to divorce his wife, **Catherine of Aragon**. The pope would not grant the divorce. Henry declared that he, not the pope, would be head of the Church of England. Henry and all of England left the Roman Catholic Church. Although the church in England changed little, the pope was no longer its authority.

Martin Luther

CAUSES OF THE REFORMATION

1 The church had become too rich, powerful, and corrupt. People had begun to challenge its authority.

2 Throughout western Europe, everyone had to pay taxes to the church in Rome, and many wanted to stop.

3 Many people resented that the church claimed rule over civil and state affairs.

4 The invention of the printing press gave more people a chance to read the Bible in Latin and, later, in their own languages. With more individuals reading and learning from books, more individuals formed their own ideas.

Catholic Reformation or Counter-Reformation

To defend itself against the Protestant movement, the Catholic church took a number of actions. These actions were called the **Catholic Reformation** or **Counter-Reformation.** These were some of the actions:

IMPORTANT EVENTS OF THE CATHOLIC REFORMATION

1 The church set up courts called the Inquisition. These courts tried to stop Protestantism by declaring Protestants heretics, or nonbelievers, and bringing them to trial. Many Jewish and Muslim believers were also tried. Those found guilty were tortured or killed.

2 The Council of Trent was set up in 1545 by Pope Paul III for bishops and cardinals to review all the teachings of the Catholic church. The council abolished the selling of indulgences but reaffirmed the pope to be head of the church with the exclusive right to interpret the Bible. The clergy was made to reform.

3 The Society of Jesus was founded by Ignatius of Loyola. Its priests were called Jesuits. The society was set up like an army, to demand complete obedience. The Jesuits were very successful in stopping converts to Protestantism as they became great teachers, opened hospitals, and worked with the poor.

4 The church published a list of books called the *Index*. These were the books good Catholics were not supposed to read.

European Expansion Overseas

The late 1400s and early 1500s began an age of exploration for European countries. They established trade routes with other countries around the African coast and began looking beyond. The Portuguese were the first to establish a good navy and train its sailors. A Portuguese prince, **Henry the Navigator**, studied pooled information of mapmakers and other travelers' information to make better ships, refine maps, and make better instruments. His work sparked the Age of Exploration. Countries sent explorers because they wanted to establish new trade routes and look for gold and gems. Other countries wanted to establish new colonies or to spread Christianity. It was in pursuit of a route to Asia that Christopher Columbus found North America.

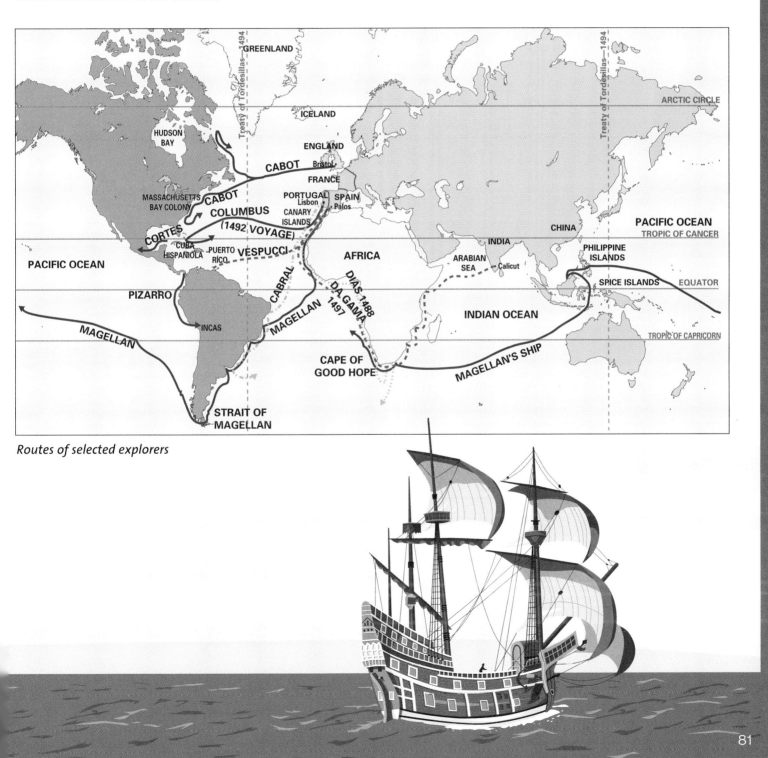

Routes of selected explorers

EARLY EUROPEAN EXPLORERS (IN CHRONOLOGICAL ORDER)

EXPLORERS	COUNTRY REPRESENTED	YEAR OF EXPLORATION	JOURNEY
Leif Erikson	Vikings (Norway)	about 1000	Newfoundland
Bartolomeu Dias	Portugal	1487–1488	First European to round Cape of Good Hope at the southern tip of Africa
Christopher Columbus	Spain	1492 1493 1498 1502	San Salvador; Cuba Puerto Rico; Jamaica; West Indies Trinidad, parts of South America
John Cabot	England	1497	Greenland; Labrador; Newfoundland
Vasco da Gama	Portugal	1497–1498	First to reach India from Europe by sea
Amerigo Vespucci	Spain, Portugal	1499–1502	South America and West Indies
Pedro Cabral	Portugal	1500	Sailed around Africa to India; Brazil
Vasco de Balboa	Spain	1513	Pacific Ocean
Juan Ponce de León	Spain	1513	Florida
Hernán Cortés	Spain	1519–1521	Aztec kingdom of Mexico
Ferdinand Magellan	Spain	1519–1522	First to sail around the world
Giovanni da Verrazano	France	1524	Eastern coast of North America
Pánfilo de Narváez	Spain	1528	Florida and Mexico
Francisco Pizarro	Spain	1533	Inca empire of Peru
Jacques Cartier	France	1535	St. Lawrence River; Canada and Quebec
Esteban and Father Marcos	Spain	1539	Zuni pueblos of New Mexico
Hernando de Soto	Spain	1539–1542	Mississippi River; American Southeast
Francisco de Coronado	Spain	1540–1542	American Southwest
Juan Rodríguez Cabrillo	Spain	1542	California
Sir Francis Drake	England	1577–1580	Around the world
Samuel de Champlain	France	1603–1609	The Great Lakes and Quebec
Henry Hudson	Netherlands	1609–1611	Hudson River and Hudson Bay

The Rise of Absolute Monarchy

During the Middle Ages, kings and queens had limited power because of the feudal lords and the church. Near the end of the Middle Ages, around 1500, the monarchs in many European countries began to expand their power. By the 1600s, some had become **absolute monarchs**, rulers with unlimited power. Their supreme power was acknowledged by lords and commoners, and the church had little power over them.

ABSOLUTE MONARCHS OF EUROPE

ENGLAND

Henry VII (1485–1509)	Responsible for establishing the king's authority over nobles.
Henry VIII (1509–1547)	Named himself head of the Church of England (see p. 79).
Elizabeth I (1558–1603)	Preserved Protestantism in England and achieved world power defeating the Spanish Armada.

FRANCE

Louis XIII (1610–1643)	Presided over the French government with Cardinal Richelieu, attaining world power for France.
Louis XIV (1643–1715)	Known as the Grand Monarch and the Sun King, he represented the height of absolutism, maintaining an extravagant court at Versailles.

SPAIN

Ferdinand and Isabella (1479–1516)	Increased royal power over the nobles and became a world power by sending explorers to conquer new lands.
Charles V (1519–1556)	Controlled Spain, the Netherlands, southern Italy, Austria, and much of central Europe as Holy Roman Emperor.
Philip II (1556–1598)	Controlled the largest empire of the time, but it declined during his reign.

RUSSIA

Peter the Great (1682–1725)	Strengthened his power by creating a strong army and crushing a revolt of the nobles. His government took control of the Russian Orthodox Church.
Catherine the Great (1762–1796)	Maintained absolute control and expanded territory.

PRUSSIA

Frederick the Great (1740–1786)	Exerted control as a powerful ruler and general who started the Seven Years' War and added part of Poland to his realm.

AUSTRIA

Maria Theresa (1740–1780)	Successfully fought off numerous attacks for her throne, ruling for 40 years.
Joseph II (1780–1790)	Put the Catholic Church under state control and weakened nobles by taxation.

The Enlightenment

The European **Age of Enlightenment** in the early 1700s brought together the ideas of the Renaissance and the **Scientific Revolution**. A group of philosophers tried to bring scientific reasoning to all parts of life. They believed that there were natural laws which, if followed, would make people happy. They were the first Europeans since ancient times to believe that free people could build a better society.

The ideas of the Enlightenment were at the root of both the French and the American revolutions. Enlightenment philosophers looked to the writings of the English philosopher **John Locke**, who opposed absolute monarchs. Locke wrote that people have a right to life, liberty, and property. He believed that people made a contract with their government to protect their natural rights.

Enlightenment philosophers in France included Voltaire, Diderot, Montesquieu, and Rousseau. The Scottish economist Adam Smith, the English geographer Captain James Cook, and Americans such as Benjamin Franklin and Thomas Jefferson were all supporters of Enlightenment ideas as well.

The French Revolution (1789)

In 1789, there were three classes of people in France—the clergy, the nobles, and the common people. They were often referred to as the **First Estate** (church), the **Second Estate** (nobles), and the **Third Estate** (common people).

There were great differences in the way the estates lived. The king had total authority. The king and the nobles lived very well and paid few taxes, while the poor struggled and paid most of the taxes. When taxes were raised, the poor often starved.

Fighting wars was expensive, and France went into debt. King **Louis XVI** called a meeting of representatives from each of the three estates to discuss raising money and new taxes. The Third Estate, the common people, tried to use this meeting to reform the government. When the king refused to give them any power, they formed the National Assembly. They met at a tennis court and agreed that they would demand a new constitution and stay together until one was written. This is known as the **Oath of the Tennis Court**.

On July 14, 1789, citizens took over the Bastille, a storehouse of ammunition and the royal prison. This sparked the beginning of the revolution.

The National Assembly put forth the **Declaration of the Rights of Man**. It was written by the **Marquis de Lafayette**, who had helped the Americans with their revolution. The National Assembly declared France a constitutional monarchy. This meant that France would be ruled by a constitution and the power of the monarch would be limited.

The revolution went on for some years and became more violent. The king and queen were tried for treason and publicly executed at the guillotine. France became a republic, but many things did not improve. The summer of 1793 through the summer of 1794 was called the **Reign of Terror** because many of the new leaders had begun to use fear and violence, executing hundreds of people each week. Only after the Reign of Terror and the death of the most ruthless leaders did the revolution end.

The guillotine was widely used during the French Revolution to behead aristocrats of the French monarchy. The device consists of a heavy blade that is dropped between two guideposts onto the neck of one sentenced to death.

CAUSES OF THE FRENCH REVOLUTION

1 The absolute control of the king and his court was an unfair system of government, a government that was also bankrupt.

2 The rich people of the First and Second estates paid few taxes, while the Third Estate, the common people, paid most of the taxes.

3 The extravagance of the rich and the misery of the poor were extreme. When the king needed even more taxes, the commoners refused.

4 Due in part to France's feudal arrangements, food was scarce. Bread, which was the main part of the peasants' diet, was very high priced by the summer of 1789.

5 The National Assembly was formed to break from the king and form a new government based on a constitution.

The Age of Napoleon (1799–1815)

Napoleon Bonaparte was a military genius and leader who created a French empire after the chaos of the revolution. He won so many battles that he became very popular with the people of France. In 1799, at the age of thirty, Napoleon overthrew the French government. He prepared a new constitution and became First Consul. He eventually ruled as a military dictator.

Napoleon restored order to France. He brought religious peace because the church accepted him. He changed the tax system and instituted new laws, called the ***Napoleonic Code***. This code made laws the same all over France and put an end to the special treatment of nobles. Napoleon then began a series of wars in order to gain new lands.

In 1804, Napoleon changed the republic into an empire and crowned himself Emperor ***Napoleon I***. At the height of his power, from 1810 to 1812, France controlled much of Europe, either directly or through the appointments of Napoleon's relatives. Four European countries joined forces in order to stop him, succeeding in 1815 at the ***Battle of Waterloo*** in Belgium. Napoleon was exiled to the small island of St. Helena until his death.

Napoleon Bonaparte

2 Russia

The Early History

In the 800s, Vikings landed in Russia and set up trade routes on the Russian rivers that led from the Baltic Sea to Constantinople, the capital of the Byzantine Empire. They ruled from two major cities—Kiev and Novgorod. Their ruler was known as the Great Prince of Kiev. Another prince, **Vladimir I**, brought Christianity to Russia. This era of Russian history is known as the **Kievian Period**.

During the European Middle Ages, Russia was invaded by the Tartars, a Mongol people from Central Asia. By 1240, Russia was part of the vast Mongol Empire. The Mongols moved the capital to Moscow, a city in the state of Muscovy. Great princes of Muscovy ruled the empire. In 1462, **Ivan III** became great prince, but he broke from the Mongols in 1480. He declared himself **czar**, which is the Slavic form of "caesar." Ivan III became known as **Ivan the Great** because he expanded Russia and created religious and political order. He set up a type of feudalism that lasted for hundreds of years. Land was granted to nobles called **boyars**; in return, these boyars gave Ivan military service. Most Russians were peasants who farmed the land. Ivan was also responsible for building great structures, including the **Kremlin**, a magnificent square in Moscow containing churches and government buildings.

Ivan's grandson, **Ivan IV**, had great victories over the Mongols early in his reign. He expanded Russia and was a just ruler. When his wife, Anastasia, died, he blamed the boyars and probably went insane. He became known as **Ivan the Terrible** because of the many common people he had killed. He even killed his own oldest son. Ivan died in 1584, and a number of civil wars followed.

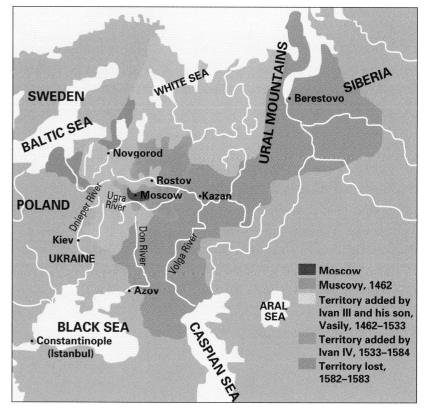

Russian-ruled territories

Russia Becomes a World Leader

The **Romanov** family took control of Russia in 1613 and remained in power for 300 years. In 1682, **Peter Romanov** became czar of Russia and ruled until 1725. His main goal was to modernize Russia, so he traveled to Europe to learn from Europeans. Upon his return, he built factories and schools, modernized the government, and improved the army. He built a new capital, St. Petersburg, and had it designed in the grand style of Europe. Peter, who is called **Peter the Great**, then set out to enlarge the empire and make Russia a major European power. He did so by defeating the Swedes and extending Russia's territory along the Baltic Sea.

    Catherine II became empress of Russia in 1762, after her husband, **Peter III**, was removed from the throne. Like Peter the Great, she admired the culture of the West and encouraged writing, art, and music throughout Russia. She also established the first school for girls and was the first to appoint women to important posts. Catherine expanded the empire greatly, taking part of Poland and part of the Ottoman Empire and eventually moving eastward to the Pacific Ocean. By the end of her reign in 1796, Russia had become a world power, and she was remembered as **Catherine the Great**.

Onion-shaped domes and colorful decorations are typical of Russian Orthodox churches.

The Modern World (1700–Present)

 Chapter 1 **After the Renaissance**

In the late eighteenth century, the growth of industry and factories made a big change in the way people lived in Europe. By the early twentieth century, more people worked in business and industry than in farming. New technology and inventions made war more terrible than ever before imagined.

The Industrial Revolution

The Industrial Revolution was the time of change when power-driven machinery replaced hand labor. It began in England in the 1760s and later spread to western Europe and the United States. During the next century, many changes were made in how things were produced. Goods began to be made in factories and a number of inventions made production faster. The steam engine, which replaced waterwheels for weaving and spinning mills, was one of the most important inventions. It enabled textile workers to make up to fifty times more cloth than was possible by hand. The textile industry was among the first to be mechanically improved. Also changed were the coal, iron, and steel industries.

The Industrial Revolution also changed the way people lived as they moved from the countryside to the city for factory jobs. The bad effects were that this created overcrowded, often unsanitary housing and miserable factory conditions. One good effect was that more new products were available for more people to own to make their lives easier. Also, the middle class grew and gained more power.

The Industrial Revolution begins in England	The first trade unions emerge to protect the rights of workers	World War I	The Russian Revolution begins	The U.S.S.R. (Union of Soviet Socialist Republics) is formed	Adolf Hitler comes to power in Germany	World War II	The United Nations is founded
1760s	**1840s**	**1914–1918**	**1917**	**1922**	**1933**	**1939–1945**	**1945**

The Rise of Unions

Factory work was brutal. Workers had to labor up to fifteen hours a day in unsafe conditions for very low pay. Children often worked ten hours a day. By the 1840s, efforts were being made to organize workers into trade unions to improve working conditions and increase pay. A **trade union** is a group of workers who join together to meet and negotiate with managers or owners for the benefit of workers. The purpose of a trade union is to give workers more power in the belief that groups of workers acting together have greater ability to win their demands than an individual acting alone. As a result of the unions' successes, a number of laws governing the treatment of laborers were passed.

The first laws passed (in Great Britain) as a result of unions:

Factory Act of 1833	Limited children ages nine to thirteen to work eight hours a day, six days a week. Children younger than nine were not allowed to work.
Mines Act of 1842	Prohibited employment of children under ten and women from working in mines.
Ten-Hour Act of 1847	Reduced working hours to ten hours a day.

INVENTIONS THAT SPURRED THE INDUSTRIAL REVOLUTION

INVENTOR	INVENTION
James Hargreaves (English)	Spinning jenny (1764). Spins a number of threads at one time.
James Watt (Scottish)	Improvement of the steam engine (1765), which advanced the Industrial Revolution.
Richard Arkwright (English)	Spinning water frame (1769). Used waterpower for spinning thread.
Samuel Crompton (English)	Spinning mule (1779). Combined spinning jenny and water frame.
Edmund Cartwright (English)	Power loom (1785). Used waterpower for weaving.
Eli Whitney (American)	Cotton gin (1793). Removed seeds from cotton.

Scottish inventor *James Watt* worked as a mathematical instrument maker at the University of Glasgow when he became interested in improving the steam engine. By 1769, he patented his new steam engine designs and, by the mid-1770s, put his idea into production.

In Watt's reciprocating steam engine, steam pushes a piston to and fro (reciprocally). The engine worked very efficiently and could be used to run large machines created for a variety of different jobs. These large machines replaced the work of humans to usher in the Industrial Revolution.

The Rise of Communism

Industrialization brought many social problems. While workers were forced to work long hours for little pay, owners were getting rich. The owners were called capitalists because they had the capital—that is, the land, the factories, and the shops.

Some people believed that this new capitalistic system was unfair. They wanted workers, not just owners, to benefit from industrialization. Their ideas became known as **socialism**.

Karl Marx, a German philosopher, and **Friedrich Engels**, the manager of an English factory, did not believe that the problems of industrialization could be solved within any existing government. They believed a new form of government called **Communism** was the answer. Under Communism, all people would own the factories and farms. The government, as representatives of the people, would own and control all property and businesses. In 1848, they published the **Communist Manifesto**, which outlined their ideas. These ideas spread rapidly, and between 1917 and 1976, more than fifteen countries around the world adopted Communism.

Karl Marx

The Russian Revolution

It was Russia that succeeded in the first Communist revolution. Russia had been in a state of unrest for many years. The workers, peasants, and many well-educated people wanted to end the absolute power of the czar and gain a say in the government. By March 1917, half the industrial workers of Petrograd (St. Petersburg) went on strike. People took to the streets and protested food shortages. Soldiers were ordered to stop the revolt, but, instead, they joined in. Czar **Nicholas II** was overthrown.

A Russian named **Vladimir Lenin** took over the government. His followers were called **Bolsheviks**. Later, they came to be called **Communists**. Civil war broke out in 1918. The czar and fifteen million other Russians were killed during the next two years. Lenin and the Bolsheviks formed the Union of Soviet Socialist Republics (U.S.S.R.) finally in 1922. It became known as the Soviet Union.

World War I (1914–1918)

Chapter **2**

World War I was the first war in which countries from all over the world took sides. Before it ended, thirty nations on five continents had been involved. When it was over, the map of Europe had changed greatly from the way it looked when the war began. Although it was called "the war to end all wars," the result would lead to another world war among many of the same nations.

World War I was the first modern war in that it was the first time that modern inventions such as airplanes, tanks, submarines, machine guns, and poison gas were widely used. It was also the bloodiest war in history up to that time.

Biplanes and tanks were introduced into battle during World War I.

A Brief History of World War I

World War I started when Archduke **Franz Ferdinand**, the future ruler of Austria-Hungary, was killed in Sarajevo on June 28, 1914. Austria-Hungary blamed the country of Serbia for his death and declared war on Serbia. This was the first act of World War I.

The countries of Europe had formed alliances with one another. An **alliance** is an agreement among nations to support one another in wartime. Russia, which had promised to support Serbia, prepared its army to fight Austria-Hungary. Germany declared war on Russia and Russia's ally, France. By August 5, all the great powers of Europe were at war. Great Britain, France, and Russia were known as the **Allies**. Germany and Austria-Hungary were called the **Central Powers**. The conflict spread to Japan and Italy on the Allied side and brought the Ottoman Empire (Turkey) among the Central Powers.

The German army quickly conquered Belgium and moved on to France. At the Battle of the Marne, the fighting stopped along an imaginary line

called the **Western Front**. It stretched from Belgium on the North Sea and looped through France before heading south, to the border of Switzerland. The war on the Western Front was fought primarily by armies living in trenches that ran along it. Despite heavy fighting over the next four years, neither side gained much territory.

The **Eastern Front** stretched 1,100 miles from the Baltic Sea to the Black Sea. The fighting here was primarily between Russia and Germany and Austria-Hungary. After the Russian government was overthrown, Russia signed a peace treaty with Germany in 1918.

Germany returned to the West. The United States entered the war in 1917 because the Germans had sunk several ships, including the *Lusitania*, a British ship with American passengers. The United States sent nearly two million soldiers to fight. After a number of bloody battles, the Allies finally forced the Germans to retreat, and the war ended in November 1918.

ALLIES	CENTRAL POWERS
Belgium	Bulgaria (from 1915)
Great Britain	Germany
France	Austria-Hungary
Italy (from 1915)	The Ottoman Empire
Japan	
Portugal	
Russia	
United States (from 1917)	

Causes of World War I

1 The industrial countries of Europe were very competitive. Germany and Austria-Hungary, in particular, wanted to increase the size of their empires.

2 Each country began to build up its supply of weapons. Germany increased the size of its navy to compete with England.

3 To protect themselves from empires, countries formed alliances. These agreements stated that if one nation were attacked, the other nations would defend it. France, Russia, and Great Britain had an alliance called the Triple Entente. Germany, Austria-Hungary, and Italy signed the Triple Alliance.

Europe before the Treaty of Versailles

4 In response to the assassination of Austrian Archduke Franz Ferdinand in Sarajevo, Bosnia, in 1914, Austria-Hungary attacked Serbia, a small country in central Europe.

5 The alliances brought many countries into the war: Russia came to the aid of Serbia. Germany then declared war on Russia. France declared war on Germany. Germany attacked Belgium. Great Britain entered the war to help Belgium and France.

6 Slavs, Czechs, and Slovaks wanted freedom from Austria-Hungary.

Results of World War I

The *Treaty of Versailles*, which ended the war, set forth these conditions:

1 Germany was to give up territory and colonies to France, Great Britain, Belgium, Denmark, and Poland.

2 To prevent Germany from starting another war, the size of its army was reduced. It was forbidden to have submarines, aircraft, armored cars, or tanks.

3 Germany accepted responsibility for starting the war and was penalized $33 billion in damages to other nations.

4 The League of Nations was formed (see p. 95).

Europe after the Treaty of Versailles

World Leaders in World War I

Georges Clemenceau. Premier of France and Minister of War during World War I. Clemenceau was nicknamed "the Tiger" because of his aggressive style.

David Lloyd George. Prime Minister of Great Britain from 1916 to 1922. Lloyd George wanted to make sure that Germany lost its navy and its empire in World War I. In the treaty that ended the war, he served as the mediator between Clemenceau, who pressed for harsh terms, and U.S. President Woodrow Wilson, who tended to be more generous.

Czar Nicholas II. Nicholas II was the last czar (king) of Russia. He was forced from the throne in 1917 when the war was not going well for Russia. He and his family were murdered in 1918 by the Bolsheviks, a revolutionary party.

Kaiser Wilhelm II. A grandson of Queen Victoria of England, Wilhelm ruled Germany from 1888 to 1918. He fled to Holland to avoid capture after Germany was defeated.

Woodrow Wilson. The twenty-eighth president of the United States, Wilson did his best to keep the United States out of the war. After the war was over, he promoted the **League of Nations** (see p. 95) to help solve disputes peacefully between countries.

Georges Clemenceau

Kaiser Wilhelm II

Czar Nicholas II

The League of Nations

U.S. President Woodrow Wilson proposed the League of Nations to prevent war by settling disputes between nations through peaceful talks. It was established in January 1920 after World War I, but the United States never joined, and the league fell apart at the start of World War II in 1939. It was officially dissolved in April 1946, when the **United Nations** began operations (see pp. 103–104).

Woodrow Wilson

The League of Nations Fails

In its early years, the League of Nations settled some disputes between nations. In some cases, it even prevented war. But it still failed, mostly because of these problems:

1 The league did not include every major nation. The United States never joined. Russia joined in 1934 but was later removed. Germany and Japan withdrew in 1933.

2 Decisions required that all countries agree, a rare occurrence.

3 The league had no power to tax its members and had to rely on voluntary contributions of its members.

4 It could not raise an army to enforce its decisions.

5 It was unable to prevent Japan from invading Manchuria (on the Asian mainland), or Italy from conquering Ethiopia (in Africa), or Bolivia and Paraguay from fighting the Chaco War.

Chapter 4 World War II (1939-1945)

A Brief History of World War II

Adolf Hitler came to power in Germany in 1933. He was a ruthless dictator who wanted to control Europe and eventually the world. In March 1938, Germany annexed Austria and took it over. Great Britain, France, and the Soviet Union protested, but did nothing.

Hitler next announced he would take the Sudetenland, a part of Czechoslovakia, by force if necessary. Czechoslovakia had an alliance with Great Britain and France that obliged them to defend Czechoslovakia if it was attacked. Britain and France wanted to avoid a war and gave the Sudetenland to Hitler, assuming he would now stop. Six months later, Hitler broke his promise and took over the rest of Czechoslovakia as well. In 1939, German troops took over Poland. Britain and France declared war.

Germany then conquered Denmark, Norway, the Netherlands, Belgium, and Luxembourg, and forced France to surrender. By 1940, Hitler controlled much of Western Europe. Germany then turned on Britain by bombing its cities. When this failed, it attacked the Soviet Union, which then joined the Allies.

The United States entered the war on the side of the Allies on December 8, 1941, the day after Japan bombed Pearl Harbor in Hawaii. By the end of the year, the United States was also at war with Germany and Italy.

After two years of war, Soviet troops defeated 300,000 Germans at Stalingrad in 1943. They pushed the German troops out of the Soviet Union and then attacked Germany.

In Western Europe, the Allies defeated Italy and were planning a massive invasion to liberate France. This secret invasion was known as D day. On June 6, 1944, the Allies, led by General **Dwight D. Eisenhower** of the United States, landed and soon freed France and Belgium. Then the Allies invaded Germany. On May 7, 1945, Germany surrendered.

The Pacific War

The war in the Pacific between the Allies and Japan continued until August 1945. The Japanese had seized Hong Kong and Singapore, and invaded the Philippines. Earlier, Japan had also seized Korea, Manchuria, and parts of China. In Southeast Asia, Japanese armies took Thailand, Burma, and the Dutch East Indies. Not until June 1942 was the United States able to stop them with the **Battle of Midway Island**. This was the turning point of the war in the Pacific and it forced the Japanese to retreat. The Japanese were losing the war, but would not surrender. In August 1945, the United States dropped **atomic bombs** on the Japanese cities of **Hiroshima** and **Nagasaki**. Japan surrendered.

By the end of the war, the total world deaths were thirty to more than fifty million, but it is impossible to guess the number of people who were wounded or disabled. There were millions of soldiers from forty countries involved in World War II, and it was fought on four continents—Europe, Asia, Africa, and North America.

ALLIES	CENTRAL POWERS
Great Britain and its empire, including Canada and India	Germany
France	Soviet Union (until 1941)
United States (from 1941)	Japan
Soviet Union (from 1941)	Italy
China	

Causes of World War II

1 The failure of the Treaty of Versailles (see p. 93) to bring lasting peace after World War I. Many Germans found the settlement insulting, thinking it punished their country unfairly.

2 Dictators in Germany, Japan, and Italy promoted a fanatical national pride, called fascism. They believed this pride was stronger than that in democratic nations where government ruled with the consent of the people.

3 The Axis powers (Germany, Japan, and Italy) wanted to conquer their neighbors. Japan wanted to create a New Order in Asia; Italy wanted to rule much of Africa; and Germany wanted to rule Europe and eventually the world. Each invaded other countries and replaced their governments with military dictatorships.

4 A terrible worldwide economic depression hit Germany especially hard because of the war reparations it was forced to make.

Dictatorships

A **dictator** is a ruler who has absolute power. A **dictatorship** is a type of government with total control over its people. The ambitions of dictators like Hitler, Stalin, and Mussolini helped steer the world into World War II.

NAZI GERMANY AND ADOLF HITLER

Adolf Hitler was originally an artist from Austria. He became involved in politics and joined the National Socialist German Workers' Party, also known as the Nazis. Hitler was a good organizer and speaker. He rose to power by combining terror with skillful **propaganda** (information spread to promote a cause or idea). His promise of jobs and the restoration of German greatness won him a large following. He became chancellor of Germany in 1933, turning the country into a brutal and terrifying dictatorship. Immediately, he started a new empire called the **Third Reich**, and took the title **führer**, which means "leader." He banned all political parties except the Nazi party, burned all books not liked by the Nazis, and cracked down on all religions that did not agree with him.

The Nazi movement was based on extreme love of country, German greatness, and hate. Hitler preached hatred of Jews and thought everyone but Germans was inferior, or not even human. These beliefs led him to kill Jews and conquer other countries to expand Germany (see Holocaust, p. 99).

STALIN'S SOVIET UNION

Josef Stalin was a revolutionary who became head of the Soviet Union and the Communist Party after Lenin's death. He was a ruthless and ambitious dictator who dealt severely with political opponents. Using the feared secret police, he forced his rivals into exile or had them killed.

Stalin ruled the Soviet Union for thirty years by fear and terror. He also modernized the country, built industry, and increased military power. He collectivized all the farms, taking them from their private owners, often after killing the landowners. He made the Soviet Union a world power again, helped defeat Nazi Germany, and took over most of eastern Europe. He died in 1953.

FASCIST RULE OF MUSSOLINI IN ITALY

Benito Mussolini was founder of the Italian **Fascist Party**. He became prime minister in 1922 and turned Italy into a dictatorship. Mussolini wanted to create an Italian empire. He invaded and captured Ethiopia in North Africa in 1935 and Albania in the Balkans in 1939. After forming an alliance with Germany, he became dependent on the Nazis and relied on their support during World War II. When the Allies moved into Italy, Mussolini was captured, but he was rescued by the Germans. Mussolini was captured again in 1945 and killed.

The Holocaust
NAZI GERMANY'S WAR AGAINST THE EUROPEAN JEWS

In one of the worst and most tragic chapters of World War II, Nazis in Germany organized the murder of millions of Jews and other people they considered enemies. This dark period is known as the *Holocaust*. (A holocaust is a disaster that wipes out life.) The Holocaust was not a dispute over land, nor was it a power struggle. It was a systematic attempt to exterminate all Jews simply because they were Jews.

Before World War II, **Adolf Hitler** (see p. 98), dreamed of a world ruled by white people he called Aryans. He built many walled prisons called concentration camps in Germany and Poland. Some were work camps where prisoners made supplies for the German army. Others were death factories. Hitler sent Jews and anyone who opposed his rule to these concentration camps.

Hitler was determined to eliminate the Jews, the biggest threat, he thought, to Aryan supremacy. He killed more than six million, a full forty percent of the world's Jewish population. Other groups, including Gypsies (Roma), the disabled, homosexuals, and political opponents of the Nazis, also became targets. Five million people from these groups lost their lives. Never before had organized murder taken place on such a horrifying scale.

In Nazi concentration camps, prisoners lived in cramped quarters with no personal possessions, except for the clothes on their backs and the dish issued them for food, if food was provided at all.

Other Leaders from World War II

Neville Chamberlain

Neville Chamberlain. Prime Minister of Great Britain at the beginning of World War II, Chamberlain was sure that Hitler could be satisfied, or appeased, by giving him more territory. In 1938, he attended a conference with Hitler, Mussolini, and the French premier during which he agreed to give Hitler the Sudetenland, part of Czechoslovakia. Chamberlain was replaced by ***Sir Winston Churchill***.

Sir Winston Churchill. Elected prime minister of Great Britain in 1940, he was an inspiring speaker, writer, and statesman who favored taking a strong stand against Hitler. His courageous leadership and defiant speeches kept British morale high during Britain's worst days of the war. In 1953, he won the Nobel Prize in literature for his six-volume memoir, *The Second World War*.

Sir Winston Churchill

Dwight D. Eisenhower. The supreme commander of the Allied forces in western Europe, General Eisenhower organized the massive Allied invasion of the French coast on D day in 1944. In 1952, he was elected president of the United States.

Dwight D. Eisenhower

Douglas MacArthur. General MacArthur was commander of U.S. forces in the southwest Pacific during World War II; later he oversaw the conversion of Japan to a peacetime economy. A man not used to taking orders, MacArthur was fired by President ***Harry S Truman*** for not following orders during the Korean War.

Douglas MacArthur

German fighter planes

Franklin Delano Roosevelt

Franklin Delano Roosevelt. The only U.S. president to be elected to four terms, Franklin Roosevelt served during two great crises in American history—the Great Depression and World War II. During his entire presidency, Roosevelt was partially paralyzed by polio. He died just three weeks before Germany surrendered.

Hideki Tojo. A Japanese military leader after World War I, Tojo was prime minister from 1941 to 1944. He wanted to build a New World Order in Asia with Japan as its leader. At the end of the war, he was executed as a war criminal.

Hideki Tojo

Harry S Truman. Vice President Harry Truman became president when Franklin Roosevelt died. It was his final decision to drop two atomic bombs on Japan, which led to its surrender. After the war, he guaranteed American aid to any country resisting Communism.

Harry S Truman

Results of World War II

1 Thirty to forty-five million people lost their lives.

2 It was the most expensive war in history, costing more than $1 trillion and leaving extensive property damage.

3 Millions of people in Europe and Asia lost their homes. Some were even unable to return to their countries. They needed help to start new lives.

4 Japan got a new constitution and a more democratic government.

5 Germany (and its capital, Berlin) was divided and eventually made into two countries. West Germany became an independent democracy. East Germany became a Communist country closely watched by the Soviet Union. (The two Germanys were reunited in 1990.)

6 The United States and the Soviet Union became the chief world powers, and their differences led to the Cold War (see p. 104), which lasted for the next forty years.

7 The United Nations was formed (see pp. 103–104).

Sherman tank

Chapter 5
The United Nations

The United Nations (UN) was founded in 1945 to maintain world peace and security. U.S. President Franklin Roosevelt, Winston Churchill of Great Britain, and Joseph Stalin of the Soviet Union worked together to form this new organization. The U.S. Congress agreed to allow the United States to join because it came to believe that future wars could be avoided through international cooperation.

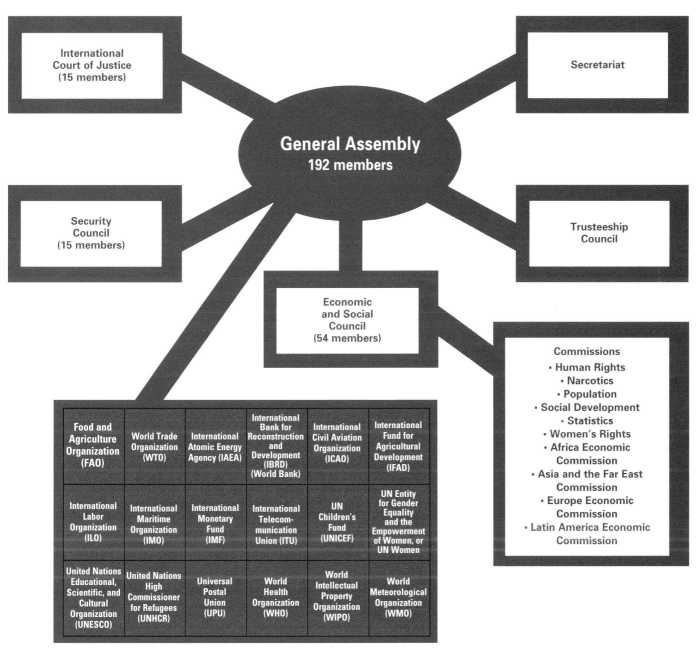

United Nations and its branches

Organization of the United Nations

The **General Assembly** is made up of all members of the UN. Each member has one vote. The General Assembly can make recommendations, but cannot give orders to act.

The **Security Council** is made up of fifteen members. There are five permanent members—the United States, Great Britain, France, Russia, and China. The other ten members are elected to two-year terms. Only the Security Council can order the UN to take action. To do this, nine of the fifteen members must vote for action. All five permanent members must also vote in favor of the action. Any one of the permanent members can veto, or reject, an issue. Along with the General Assembly, the Security Council meets in New York City.

The **Secretariat** consists of the **Secretary-General** and his or her staff. They are responsible for the daily running of the organization. The Secretary-General is appointed by the General Assembly for a five-year term.

The **International Court of Justice** is made up of fifteen judges who decide cases by majority vote. When nations submit their cases to the court, they agree to accept its decision. The court meets in The Hague, Netherlands.

The Cold War

Following World War II, the Soviets remained in most of the countries they freed, including Poland, Hungary, Czechoslovakia, Bulgaria, and East Germany. The Soviet Union also supported governments in the countries friendly to them. This led to tension between the Soviet Union and the major non-Communist nations, especially the United States. British Prime Minister Winston Churchill declared, "An iron curtain has descended across the continent" (meaning Europe). This tension, called the **Cold War**, lasted from the 1940s to the 1980s, as both the Soviet Union and the United States sought to protect their interests and gain allies around the world. It ended with the destruction of the Berlin Wall in 1989 and the breakup of the Soviet Union in 1991.

chapter **6**

Events Since World War II

1945:   The **Cold War** begins.

1946:   The Philippines gain independence from United States.

War breaks out in Indochina between colonial France and Vietnamese Communists and Nationalists.

1947–1948:   Soviet support helps Communist dictatorships seize power across eastern Europe.

Pakistan and India gain independence.

1948:   The State of Israel is founded.

South Africa makes apartheid law.

1949:   **North Atlantic Treaty Organization** (NATO), comprised of Western democracies, is formed.

The members are the United States; Canada; Iceland; Norway; Britain; the Netherlands; Denmark; Belgium; France; Luxembourg; Portugal; Italy; Greece and Turkey (both joined in 1952); West Germany (joined in 1955); Spain (joined in 1982); Czech Republic, Hungary, and Poland (joined in 1999); Bulgaria, Estonia, Latvia, Lithuania, Romania, Slovakia, and Slovenia (joined in 2004); and Albania and Croatia (joined in 2009).

Mao Zedong establishes People's Republic of China.

Nationalists under **Chiang Kai-shek** flee to Taiwan.

The Soviets build an atomic bomb.

1950:   The **Korean War** begins when the Communist army of North Korea invades South Korea.

U.S. President **Harry S Truman** sends troops to South Korea's defense and asks for the backing of the United Nations.

General **Douglas MacArthur** leads the UN troops to stop the North Koreans.

1952:   Britain's **King George VI** dies and **Queen Elizabeth II** is crowned.

1953:   **Dwight D. Eisenhower** becomes president of the United States.

The Korean War ends in stalemate.

Stalin dies in the Soviet Union.

1954: The French leave Indochina.

Vietnam divides into the Communist North and non-Communist South.

1955: The **Warsaw Pact**, comprised of Communist dictatorships, is formed in response to NATO.

The members are the Soviet Union, Albania, Bulgaria, Czechoslovakia, East Germany, Hungary, Poland, and Romania.

1956: Hungarians revolt against Communist rule, but are stopped by Soviet troops.

Martin Luther King, Jr., rises as leader of the nonviolent civil rights movement in the United States.

Egypt nationalizes the Suez Canal.

With British and French support, Israel recaptures the canal.

UN peacekeeping forces step in to give the canal back to Egypt.

1957: The Soviet Union launches the first satellite, **Sputnik**, into space.

The modern nation of Ghana wins independence from Great Britain, the first of thirty-eight new countries on the African map by 1968.

1958: The Soviet Union gives a loan to Egypt to build the Aswan Dam on the Nile River.

Nikita Khrushchev becomes premiere of the Soviet Union.

1959: **Fidel Castro** overthrows the Fulgencio Batista government of Cuba and becomes dictator.

1960: **John F. Kennedy** is elected president of the United States.

Senegal under Leopold Senghor becomes one of Africa's few true democracies.

1961: Communists build the Berlin Wall across the divided city of Berlin in East Germany to prevent citizens from fleeing to the West.

U.S. Bay of Pigs invasion fails to free Cuba of the Castro dictatorship.

1962: The Soviet Union puts nuclear missiles in Cuba and triggers fears of nuclear war with the United States.

Algeria wins independence from France after a seventy-year war.

1963: U.S. President John F. Kennedy is assassinated.

Lyndon B. Johnson becomes president.

1964: The U.S. Civil Rights Act makes racial discrimination illegal.

China explodes its first atomic bomb.

1965: President Johnson sends U.S. combat troops to Vietnam.

1966: *Indira Gandhi* becomes Indian prime minister.

1967: In retaliation for Egypt's takeover of the Gulf of Aqaba, Israel launches the *Six-Day War*, in which it is victorious.

Israeli troops remain in the Sinai Peninsula, taken from Egypt, the Golan Heights, taken from Syria, and the West Bank, taken from Jordan.

Israel takes complete control of Jerusalem.

1968: *Martin Luther King, Jr*., and Senator *Robert Kennedy* are assassinated.

Richard Nixon is elected president of the United States.

Warsaw Pact troops take over Prague, the capital of Czechoslovakia, putting down its reforms of Communism.

Fighting breaks out in Northern Ireland between Protestants and Roman Catholics.

1969: *Neil Armstrong* is the first U.S. astronaut to walk on the moon.

1970: Socialist *Salvador Allende* is elected president of Chile.

1971: East Pakistan wins independence from Pakistan and becomes the nation of Bangladesh.

Dictator *Idi Amin* seizes power in Uganda.

500,000 people die as a result of his brutality and the revenge that follows after he is driven into exile in 1979.

1972: Ceylon becomes the Republic of Sri Lanka.

U.S. president *Richard Nixon* visits China.

Watergate break-in starts the chain of events that lead to the end of the Nixon presidency.

Palestinian group *Black September* terrorists kill Israeli athletes at the Olympics in Munich, Germany.

Britain takes control of Northern Ireland after years of violence between Protestants and Catholics.

Philippine president *Ferdinand Marcos* seizes power as dictator.

1973:   United States pulls troops out of Vietnam.

Arab forces attack Israel on the Jewish holiday of Yom Kippur.

After heavy casualties on both sides, an uneasy truce is called.

Organization of Petroleum Exporting Countries (OPEC) protests U.S. support for Israel and sharply cuts oil production, triggering a crisis in the United States.

General **Augusto Pinochet** overthrows the Allende government in Chile.

Allende dies.

1974:   **Richard Nixon** resigns.

Gerald Ford becomes president of the United States.

1976:   **Jimmy Carter** is elected president of the United States.

Mao Zedong of China dies.

The Second Revolution begins to open agriculture and industry to individuals in China.

1978:   At Camp David, Maryland, Egypt's **Anwar Sadat** agrees to recognize Israel's right to exist and Israel's **Menachem Begin** agrees to return the Sinai Peninsula to Egypt.

Deng Xiaoping becomes the leader of China.

1979:   **Margaret Thatcher** is named the first female prime minister of England.

Iran holds U.S. citizens hostage.

The United States establishes diplomatic relations with China.

Muslim Fundamentalists take over Iran.

1980:   Black majority rule comes to Zimbabwe.

Ronald Reagan is elected president of the United States.

Eight-year war between Iran and Iraq begins.

1981:   Egyptian president **Anwar Sadat** is assassinated by Muslim Fundamentalists.

1983:   **Raul Alfonsin** is elected president of Argentina in the first free election there in forty years.

1984:   **Indira Gandhi** is killed.

Rajiv Gandhi, her son, succeeds her as prime minister of India.

1985:   **Mikhail Gorbachev** is named general secretary of the Communist Party of the Soviet Union.

1985–1990: *Gorbachev* institutes policies of *perestroika* (restructuring) and *glasnost* (openness) in the Soviet Union.

1986: President and dictator *Ferdinand Marcos* flees the Philippines.

Corazon Aquino becomes president.

1987: The Iran-Contra hearings explore possible White House crimes in connection with aiding Nicaraguan Contras (counter revolutionaries).

1988: Pakistani president *Zia-ul-Haq* is killed.

Benazir Bhutto becomes prime minister.

George H. W. Bush is elected president of the United States.

Iran-Iraq war ends with Iraq under *Saddam Hussein* victorious over Muslim Fundamentalists.

Palestine Liberation Organization (PLO) recognizes Israel's right to exist.

1989: The Berlin Wall falls, signaling the end of the Cold War.

1989–1990: Communist dictatorships fall throughout eastern Europe now that it is clear Gorbachev will not back them up by military force.

The United States and international military force fight to keep Iraq out of Kuwait which eventually erupts into the Persian Gulf War.

1991: A military coup against Gorbachev fails in August, but he resigns.

The Soviet Union dissolves into many separate countries.

Boris Yeltsin is elected president of Russia.

Civil war breaks out in Yugoslavia; Yugoslavia is broken into Bosnia and Herzegovina, Croatia, Macedonia, Serbia and Montenegro, and Slovenia.

1992: *William Jefferson Clinton* is elected president of the United States.

1993: Czechoslovakia divides into two countries, the Czech Republic and Slovakia.

The *General Agreement on Tariffs and Trade* (GATT) establishes the World Trade Organization to make trade easier between nations, while the *North American Free Trade Agreement* (NAFTA) eases trade barriers between Canada, the United States, and Mexico.

1994: *Nelson Mandela* becomes the first elected black president of South Africa.

Palestinian Liberation Organization (PLO) chairman *Yasir Arafat* enters Palestinian soil for the first time in twenty-seven years as a result of a new accord with Israel.

1995: A peace accord is signed in Dayton, Ohio, ending a nearly four-year civil war in Bosnia and Herzegovina.

Israeli leader **Yitzhak Rabin** and PLO leader Yasir Arafat agree that Israel will pull out of the West Bank and that Palestinians will rule themselves there. In November, Rabin is assassinated by an Israeli extremist.

1996: In Russia's presidential elections, **Boris Yeltsin** narrowly defeats Communist candidate **Gennadi Zyuganov**, showing that Russians aren't happy with the slow speed of democratic reforms, but that they are not unhappy enough to return to a Communist political system.

1997: After more than 150 years as a British colony, Hong Kong is restored to Chinese rule on July 1.

1998: India and Pakistan, neighbors and longtime enemies, alarm the world by conducting nuclear tests; many countries oppose the testing, and international sanctions are imposed on the two countries.

1999: The European Union's new currency, the euro, becomes the official currency for 11 countries throughout Europe.

However, it was not until 2002 that the circulation of paper money and coins began.

Canada creates a new territory for native Inuits called Nunavut. This land was formerly part of the Northwest Territories.

Vladimir Putin becomes president of Russia.

2000: **George W. Bush** is elected president of the United States.

Kim Jong Il of North Korea and **Kim Dae Jung** of South Korea meet and sign an agreement to work toward unification of Korea.

Kim Dae Jung wins the Nobel Peace Prize for his efforts.

2001: On **September 11**, terrorists destroy the World Trade Center in New York City and significantly damage the Pentagon in Washington, D.C.

"Operation Enduring Freedom" begins as U.S. soldiers are sent to Afghanistan to fight the Taliban and Al Qaeda.

2002: American **Steve Fossett** completes the first solo around-the-world balloon flight consisting of 19,428 miles.

Yugoslavia is renamed Serbia and Montenegro. In 2006, Montenegro declares its independence from Serbia.

2003: The United States, Great Britain, and Spain begin a military campaign called *"Operation Iraqi Freedom"* that leads to the removal of the dictator **Saddam Hussein**.

2004: A massive earthquake in the Indian Ocean sets off a tsunami that kills 230,000 people in fifteen countries.

Facebook is launched in California, beginning a new era of social media.

2005: Iraq holds its first free elections in fifty years.

Terrorists bomb London subways in response to Britain's involvement in the Iraq war.

2006: Former Iraqi dictator Saddam Hussein is convicted of "crimes against humanity" and executed.

The United Nations sends a peacekeeping force into the Darfur region of the Sudan, where an ongoing civil war has resulted in more than 200,000 deaths.

2007: U.S. astronaut Sunita Williams ends a 195-day stay aboard the International Space Station—a new record for a female astronaut.

2008: The collapse of a number of major U.S. businesses and financial institutions leads to a worldwide financial crisis.

Kosovo declares independence from Serbia.

Dmitry Medvedev is elected president of Russia.

Barack Obama is elected president of the United States.

2009: As the Taliban gains strength once again, the U.S. sends 30,000 more troops to Afghanistan.

Judge **Sonia Sotomayor** becomes the U.S. Supreme Court's first Hispanic justice.

2010: A massive earthquake in Port-au-Prince, Haiti, destroys much of the city and kills more than 200,000 people.

U.S. combat troops withdraw from Iraq.

In Myanmar, also called Burma, democracy campaigner and Nobel Peace Prize laureate Aung San Suu Kyi is released after more than seven years under house arrest.

The Deepwater Horizon oil platform explodes in the Gulf of Mexico, resulting in one of the largest oil spills in history. Also known as the BP Oil Spill, more than 200 million gallons of crude oil escaped before being capped three months later.

American scientists create the first functional synthetic genome.

Current Events

World Terrorism

On the morning of September 11, 2001, Americans watched in horror as the World Trade Center towers in New York City were attacked and destroyed, killing thousands of people; in 1995, the Japanese subway system was contaminated with poison gas, killing twelve and sending 5,000 people to hospitals; there were 328 victims when an Air India aircraft was exploded by terrorists in 1985. All of these are acts of terrorism that were committed around the world.

The term **terrorism** is defined as "the unlawful use of force or violence against people or property to force a government, or civilians, to further political, religious, or social objectives." Terrorism always attracts a great deal of attention because of its sudden, often unexpected, occurrence. And it almost always results in death.

World terrorism as we know it today is often thought to have begun with the hostage crisis at the Munich Olympics in 1972 when a Palestinian group known as **Black September** kidnapped Israeli athletes inside the Olympic Village. The Palestinian group demanded the release of Palestinian prisoners held in Israel in return for the hostages they held in Munich. The Israeli government refused the terrorists' demands. The failed rescue resulted in all the athletes' deaths, shocking the world.

The **Irish Republican Army**'s (IRA) use of terrorism captured world attention for many years. They used violence to get attention from the British government in order to try to get them to leave Northern Ireland. The IRA also used terrorist activities to force the government to negotiate with them.

Conflicts and terrorist activities remain a problem around the globe. Palestine and Israel continue today to conduct terrorist activities against each other in the struggle for land and peace in the Middle East. The Basques in Spain struggle for independence, and many other groups around the world resort to terrorism to make demands of people and governments.

Since the September 11 attacks on America, the threat of terrorism is affecting the world. President George W. Bush declared that the United States would wage war against terrorism wherever it exists. The United States also instituted a Department of Homeland Security and works with governments around the world on a system of terror alerts. Many countries have instituted anti-terrorist police forces to prevent attacks, as well as track down terrorist suspects.

On May 1, 2011, upon orders from President Barack Obama, an elite team of Navy SEALs stormed a fortified compound in Pakistan and killed **Osama bin Laden**, the leader of al Qaeda and the most wanted man in the world. The troops identified bin Laden's body and then buried him at sea.

Much is being done to combat terrorism, but it will likely continue to be an international problem for years to come. The threat of terrorism has caused the world to become more watchful.

The Internet or the "Global Information System"

The Internet is a network of computers that are connected to one another. It is often defined as a "global information system" because its connection of computers from all around the world allows us to retrieve information from many countries.

The idea for the Internet was conceived as early as the 1920s, but it was not until the 1990s that the Internet became a reality. The first major set of connections was called Advanced Research Projects Agency (ARPA). These early Internet connections were set up in 1969 between universities for the purpose of research and between divisions of the government for linking military activities. But it was not until the 1990s that the Internet became well known.

The two most popular applications of the Internet are electronic mail, also called e-mail, and the World Wide Web. The first e-mail was sent in 1976 by Queen Elizabeth II of Great Britain. Since that time, this form of communication has grown rapidly as more and more people have computers.

In 1989, a new technique was developed for distributing information on the Internet that was called the World Wide Web. This technique allowed the user to connect from one document to another at different sites on the Internet. This eventually led to the development of Web sites all around the world. The bulk of the Web today is made up of private networking facilities in educational and research institutions, businesses, and in government organizations across the globe.

The Internet has exploded in popularity on a worldwide scale. The number of Internet users has grown to almost 2 billion. New technologies such as instant messaging, video conferencing, file sharing, and Internet telephony have changed the way we communicate and do business. Social networking Web sites such as Facebook and Twitter allow users to stay in constant contact and share information almost instantly. Computers themselves have changed. Through wireless networking, we can access the Internet almost anywhere, via laptops, notebooks, and cellular phones. Personal computers have transformed the world. The growth of the Internet has been instrumental in this change.

The International Space Station

The dream of journeying from Earth to the moon or Mars has been a goal of most space exploration. Space stations create a way to have humans in space on a permanent basis. The Russians launched the first space station, *Salyut*, in 1971. *Skylab* was the initial U.S. space station, in 1973.

Russia's *Mir* space station, the most successful space station, was launched on February 20, 1986. It completed more than 86,325 trips around the Earth. In its fifteen years in orbit, cosmonauts and astronauts from fifteen countries lived on the station and performed experiments and conducted research. The U.S. sent numerous space shuttles to *Mir* to work with the Russians.

In 1993, the United States, Russia, and sixteen international partners agreed to build a joint facility that became known as the International Space Station (ISS). The International Space Station is the largest and most complex international scientific project in history.

Upon completion in 2011, the ISS will be more than four times as large as the Russian *Mir* space station and will consist of sixteen pressurized modules, including labs, living quarters, and docking compartments—more than any spacecraft ever built.

The first phase of the International Space Station, the Shuttle–*Mir* Program, began in 1995 and involved more than two years of continuous stays by astronauts aboard the Russian *Mir* space station. The first crew to live aboard the International Space Station was in 2000 and was commanded by U.S. astronaut Bill Shepherd. It included Russian cosmonauts Yuri Gidzenko and Sergei Krikalev. Ten years after that first crew arrived, in November 2010, the ISS became the longest continuously inhabited spacecraft.

Chronology of Space Flight Firsts

1957:   The first satellite, called *Sputnik I* (U.S.S.R.), is launched into space.

1957:   Laika, a Russian dog, is the first animal ever to travel into space on *Sputnik II*.

1959:   *Luna 3* (U.S.S.R.), the first successful space probe (unmanned space vehicle equipped with cameras), flies past the moon and sends back the first picture of the moon's far side.

1961:   Russian **Yuri Gagarin** becomes the first person to travel into space, circling the earth one time in *Vostok I*.

1961:   The first American in space is **Alan Shepard**.

1962:   *Mariner 3* (U.S.), the first planetary space probe, flies past Venus and sends back photographs.

1962:   The first American to orbit in space is **John Glenn**, who traveled around the Earth three times.

1963:   **Valentina Tereshkova**, a Soviet cosmonaut, becomes the first woman to travel into space.

1965:   The first person to walk in space is Soviet cosmonaut **Alexei Leonov**.

1969:   American **Neil Armstrong** becomes the first person to walk on the moon.

1971:   The first space station, *Salyut I* (U.S.S.R.), goes into orbit.

1973:   The first U.S. manned space station, *Skylab 2*, is launched.

1981:   U.S. space shuttle *Columbia* makes its first test flight into space.

1983:   The first U.S. woman, **Sally Ride**, is launched into space aboard the first *Challenger* space shuttle.

1990:   Hubble Telescope is launched from the U.S. to photograph the universe for approximately fifteen years.

2000:   Expedition One, the first crew, arrives aboard the International Space Station.

2001:   Russian space station *Mir* completes its fifteenth year in orbit on February 20. It is deorbited in March.

2003:   China launches its first manned space mission.

2004:   SpaceShipOne is the first privately built craft to go into outer space.

2010:   The International Space Station becomes the longest continuously inhabited spacecraft.

Appendix: The World In Focus

Area & Population: Taken together, these figures allow you to calculate population density (population divided by area)—the average number of people who live on each square mile of land.

Urban Population: The percent of a country's total population living in urban areas.

Political System & Head of Government: Presidential-parliamentary systems split authority between a president (head of state) and a prime minister (head of government). The more powerful of the two is listed.

Date of Origin: The year in which a country declared independence, won control of its affairs, or established its present boundaries.
Literacy Rate: The percent of people who can read and write (male/female[1]).

Per Capita GDP: The value in U.S. dollars of all goods and services produced within a country in one year (its gross domestic product), divided by its population. It is one way to gauge a nation's wealth.

COUNTRY	AREA (SQ MI)	URBAN POP. %	CAPITAL	LANGUAGES	POLITICAL SYSTEM & HEAD OF GOVERNMENT	DATE OF ORIGIN	LITERACY RATE (%)	PER CAPITA GDP
	POPULATION	POP. RISE %/YEAR				% OF POP. UNDER 15	LIFE EXPECTANCY	HDI
France	212,934	77	Paris	French, regional dialects	Presidential-parliamentary democracy; President Nicolas Sarkozy	486	99/99	$32,600
	63,000,000	0.4				18	78/85	0.961

Percent of Population Increase: The birth rate minus the death rate of a country. Population growth in poor countries tends to be higher than in wealthier ones.

Languages Spoken: We show only major languages. Some 7,000 languages are spoken in the world, not counting local dialects. About 12 percent of all people speak Mandarin Chinese—more than double any other language.

Percent of Population Under Age 15: Developing countries with a high percentage of young people may have trouble providing enough jobs, schools, and food.

Life Expectancy: The age to which a newborn can expect to live. The first number is for males, the second for females.

HDI (Human Development Index): This number measures economic and human well-being on a scale of 0 to 1. It combines life expectancy, literacy, and purchasing power into one figure.

[1]When breakdown by gender is not available, a single figure represents the population as a whole.

NORTH AMERICA

COUNTRY	AREA (SQ MI) / POPULATION	URBAN POP. % / POP. RISE %/YEAR	CAPITAL	LANGUAGES	POLITICAL SYSTEM & HEAD OF GOVERNMENT	DATE OF ORIGIN / % OF POP. UNDER 15	LITERACY RATE (%) / LIFE EXPECTANCY	PER CAPITA GDP / HDI
Antigua and Barbuda	170 / 100,000	31 / 0.9	St. John's	English, English patois (PAH-twah)	Parliamentary democracy; Prime Minister Baldwin Spencer	1981 / 28	86 / 73/77	$17,800 / 0.868
Bahamas	5,359 / 300,000	83 / 0.9	Nassau	English, Creole	Parliamentary democracy; Prime Minister Hubert Ingraham	1973 / 26	95/97 / 71/77	$29,700 / 0.856
Barbados	166 / 300,000	38 / 0.5	Bridgetown	English, Bajan	Parliamentary democracy; Prime Minister David Thompson	1966 / 19	99/99 / 71/76	$17,700 / 0.903
Belize	8,865 / 300,000	51 / 2.3	Belmopan	English, Spanish, Mayan, Garifuna	Parliamentary democracy; Prime Minister Dean Barrow	1981 / 37	77/77 / 71/74	$8,300 / 0.772
Canada	3,849,670 / 34,100,000	80 / 0.4	Ottawa	English, French	Parliamentary democracy; Prime Minister Stephen Harper	1867 / 17	99/99 / 78/83	$38,200 / 0.966
Costa Rica	19,730 / 4,600,000	59 / 1.3	San José	Spanish, English	Presidential-legislative democracy; President Laura Chinchilla	1821 / 23	95/95 / 77/82	$10,900 / 0.854
Cuba	42,803 / 11,200,000	75 / 0.3	Havana	Spanish	Communist one-party state; President Raúl Castro	1902 / 18	99/99 / 76/80	$9,700 / 0.863
Dominica	290 / 100,000	73 / 0.7	Roseau	English, French patois	Parliamentary democracy; Prime Minister Roosevelt Skerrit	1978 / 23	94/94 / 72/78	$10,200 / 0.814
Dominican Republic	18,815 / 9,900,000	67 / 1.7	Santo Domingo	Spanish	Presidential-legislative democracy; President Leonel Fernández	1844 / 32	87/87 / 69/75	$8,300 / 0.777
El Salvador	8,124 / 6,200,000	63 / 1.4	San Salvador	Spanish, Nahua	Presidential-legislative democracy; President Mauricio Funes	1821 / 33	83/80 / 67/76	$7,200 / 0.747
Grenada	131 / 100,000	31 / 0.8	St. George's	English, French patois	Parliamentary democracy; Prime Minister Tillman Thomas	1974 / 31	96 / 68/72	$10,300 / 0.813
Guatemala	42,042 / 14,400,000	47 / 2.8	Guatemala City	Spanish, Amerindian dialects	Presidential-legislative democracy; President Álvaro Colom Caballeros	1821 / 42	75/63 / 66/73	$5,100 / 0.704
Haiti	10,714 / 9,800,000	48 / 1.8	Port-au-Prince	French, Creole	Presidential-legislative democracy (transitional); President René Préval	1804 / 37	55/51 / 59/62	$1,300 / 0.532
Honduras	43,278 / 7,600,000	50 / 2.3	Tegucigalpa	Spanish, Amerindian dialects	Presidential-parliamentary democracy in transition after coup; President Porfirio Lobo	1821 / 38	80/80 / 70/75	$4,100 / 0.732
Jamaica	4,243 / 2,700,000	52 / 1.2	Kingston	English, English patois	Parliamentary democracy; Prime Minister Bruce Golding	1962 / 28	84/92 / 68/75	$8,400 / 0.766
Mexico	756,062 / 110,600,000	77 / 1.4	Mexico City	Spanish, Mayan, other indigenous languages	Presidential-legislative democracy; President Felipe Calderón	1810 / 29	87/85 / 74/79	$13,200 / 0.854
Nicaragua	50,193 / 6,000,000	56 / 1.8	Managua	Spanish, English, Amerindian dialects	Presidential-legislative democracy; President Daniel Ortega	1821 / 35	67/68 / 69/73	$2,800 / 0.699
Panama	29,158 / 3,500,000	64 / 1.6	Panama City	Spanish, English	Presidential-legislative democracy; President Ricardo Martinelli	1903 / 30	93/91 / 73/78	$12,100 / 0.840
Saint Kitts and Nevis	139 / 100,000	32 / 0.7	Basseterre	English, English patois	Parliamentary democracy; Prime Minister Denzil Douglas	1983 / 24	98 / 71/76	$14,700 / 0.838
Saint Lucia	239 / 200,000	28 / 0.7	Castries	English, French patois	Parliamentary democracy; Prime Minister Stephenson King	1979 / 25	90/91 / 71/76	$10,900 / 0.821
Saint Vincent and the Grenadines	151 / 100,000	40 / 0.9	Kingstown	English, English patois	Parliamentary democracy; Prime Minister Ralph Gonsalves	1979 / 28	96/96 / 70/74	$10,200 / 0.772
Trinidad and Tobago	1,981 / 1,300,000	12 / 0.6	Port-of-Spain	English, Hindi, French patois, Spanish	Parliamentary democracy; Prime Minister Kamla Persad-Bissessar	1962 / 25	99/98 / 66/73	$21,300 / 0.837
United States	3,717,796 / 309,600,000	79 / 0.6	Washington, D.C.	English, Spanish, others	Presidential-legislative democracy; President Barack Obama	1776 / 20	99/99 / 75/80	$46,000 / 0.956

SOURCES: FOR AREA, POPULATION, URBAN POPULATION, ANNUAL POPULATION INCREASE, PERCENT OF POPULATION UNDER 15 YEARS, AND LIFE EXPECTANCY: 2010 WORLD POPULATION DATA SHEET (POPULATION REFERENCE BUREAU) • FOR CAPITAL, MAJOR LANGUAGES, DATE OF ORIGIN, LITERACY RATE, AND PER CAPITA GDP: THE WORLD FACTBOOK 2010 (CENTRAL INTELLIGENCE AGENCY) • FOR POLITICAL SYSTEMS: BASED ON INFORMATION FROM FREEDOM IN THE WORLD, AN ANNUAL PUBLICATION OF FREEDOM HOUSE (A NONPROFIT HUMAN-RIGHTS ORGANIZATION) AND ITS WEB SITE (FREEDOMHOUSE.ORG); NEWS ACCOUNTS; WORLD BOOK ENCYCLOPEDIA; THE U.S. STATE DEPARTMENT AND ITS WEB SITE (STATE.GOV); AND BBC NEWS COUNTRY PROFILES • FOR HEADS OF GOVERNMENT: BASED ON INFORMATION FROM THE GEOCITIES "RULERS" WEB SITE (RULERS.ORG), THE STATE DEPARTMENT AND ITS WEB SITE, THE WORLD FACTBOOK 2010, AND NEWS ACCOUNTS • FOR HDI: HUMAN DEVELOPMENT REPORT 2009 (UNITED NATIONS DEVELOPMENT PROGRAM) • FOR KOSOVO: WORLD BOOK ENCYCLOPEDIA, THE WORLD FACTBOOK 2010, AND THE STATE DEPARTMENT WEB SITE

DATA COMPILED AND EDITED BY BRYAN BROWN, KATHY WILMORE, VERONICA MAJEROL, MARY HARVEY, AND STEVEN WISHNIA; DATA CONFIRMED AS OF OCTOBER 4, 2010.

COUNTRY	AREA (SQ MI) POPULATION	URBAN POP. % POP. RISE %/YEAR	CAPITAL	LANGUAGES	POLITICAL SYSTEM & HEAD OF GOVERNMENT	DATE OF ORIGIN % OF POP. UNDER 15	LITERACY RATE (%) LIFE EXPECTANCY	PER CAPITA GDP HDI
Argentina	1,073,514	91	Buenos Aires	Spanish, English, Italian, German, French	Presidential-legislative democracy; President Cristina Fernández de Kirchner	1816	97/97	$13,400
	40,500,000	1.0				26	72/79	0.866
Bolivia	424,162	65	La Paz *and* Sucre	Spanish, Quechua, Aymara	Presidential-legislative democracy; President Evo Morales	1825	93/81	$4,700
	10,400,000	2.0				37	64/68	0.729
Brazil	3,300,154	84	Brasília	Portuguese, Amerindian dialects	Presidential-legislative democracy; President Dilma Rousseff	1822	88/89	$10,100
	193,300,000	1.0				27	69/77	0.813
Chile	292,135	87	Santiago	Spanish	Presidential-legislative democracy; President Sebastián Piñera	1810	96/96	$14,600
	17,100,000	0.9				24	76/82	0.878
Colombia	439,734	75	Bogotá	Spanish	Presidential-legislative democracy; President Juan Manuel Santos	1810	90/91	$9,200
	45,500,000	1.4				30	71/78	0.807
Ecuador	109,483	65	Quito	Spanish, Quechua, Amerindian dialects	Presidential-legislative democracy; President Rafael Correa	1822	92/90	$7,500
	14,200,000	1.6				31	72/78	0.806
Guyana	83,000	28	Georgetown	English, Amerindian dialects	Presidential-parliamentary democracy; President Bharrat Jagdeo	1966	92/92	$6,500
	800,000	1.6				33	62/70	0.729
Paraguay	157,046	58	Asunción	Spanish, Guarani	Presidential-legislative democracy; President Fernando Lugo	1811	95/93	$4,600
	6,500,000	1.9				34	70/74	0.761
Peru	496,224	76	Lima	Spanish, Quechua, Aymara	Presidential-legislative democracy; President Alan García	1821	96/89	$8,500
	29,500,000	1.6				31	71/76	0.806
Suriname	63,039	67	Paramaribo	Dutch, English, Sranang, Tongo, Hindustani, Javanese	Parliamentary democracy; President Dési Bouterse	1975	92/87	$9,500
	500,000	1.3				30	65/73	0.769
Uruguay	68,498	94	Montevideo	Spanish, Portuñol	Presidential-legislative democracy; President José Mujica	1825	98/98	$12,600
	3,400,000	0.5				23	72/80	0.865
Venezuela	352,143	88	Caracas	Spanish, Amerindian dialects	Presidential-legislative democracy; President Hugo Chávez	1811	93/93	$13,000
	28,800,000	1.6				30	71/77	0.844

EUROPE

COUNTRY	AREA (SQ MI) POPULATION	URBAN POP. % POP. RISE %/YEAR	CAPITAL	LANGUAGES	POLITICAL SYSTEM & HEAD OF GOVERNMENT	DATE OF ORIGIN % OF POP. UNDER 15	LITERACY RATE (%) LIFE EXPECTANCY	PER CAPITA GDP HDI
Albania	11,100	49	Tirana	Albanian, Greek	Presidential-parliamentary democracy; Prime Minister Sali Berisha	1912	99/98	$6,400
	3,200,000	0.5				25	72/79	0.818
Andorra	174	90	Andorra la Vella	Catalan, French, Castilian, Portuguese	Presidential-parliamentary democracy; Executive Council President Jaume Bartumeu Cassany	1278	99/99	$44,900
	100,000	0.7				14	NA	0.934
Austria	32,378	67	Vienna	German	Parliamentary democracy; Chancellor Werner Faymann	1156	98	$39,200
	8,400,000	0				15	78/83	0.955
Belarus	80,154	74	Minsk	Belarusian, Russian, others	Presidential dictatorship; President Aleksandr Lukashenko	1991	99/99	$12,500
	9,500,000	−0.3				15	65/76	0.826
Belgium	11,787	99	Brussels	Flemish, French, German	Parliamentary democracy; Prime Minister Yves Leterme	1830	99/99	$36,800
	10,800,000	0.2				17	77/82	0.953
Bosnia and Herzegovina[2]	19,741	46	Sarajevo	Serbo-Croatian	Presidential-parliamentary (transitional); rotating Chairman of the Presidency[2]	1992	99/94	$6,400
	3,800,000	0				16	72/77	0.812
Bulgaria	42,822	71	Sofia	Bulgarian, others	Parliamentary democracy; Prime Minister Boiko Borisov	1908	99/98	$12,500
	7,500,000	−0.4				14	70/77	0.840
Croatia	21,830	56	Zagreb	Serbo-Croatian	Presidential-parliamentary democracy; Prime Minister Jadranka Kosor	1991	99/97	$17,500
	4,400,000	−0.2				15	72/79	0.871
Czech Republic	30,448	74	Prague	Czech, Slovak	Parliamentary democracy; Prime Minister Petr Nečas	1993	99/99	$24,900
	10,500,000	0.1				14	74/80	0.903
Denmark	16,637	72	Copenhagen	Danish, Greenlandic, Faroese, German	Parliamentary democracy; Prime Minister Lars Løkke Rasmussen	900s	99/99	$36,000
	5,500,000	0.1				19	76/81	0.955

[2]Bosnia and Herzegovina has a collective presidency that alternates among three members (one Croat, one Bosniak Muslim, and one Serb).

COUNTRY	AREA (SQ MI) POPULATION	URBAN POP. % POP. RISE %/YEAR	CAPITAL	LANGUAGES	POLITICAL SYSTEM & HEAD OF GOVERNMENT	DATE OF ORIGIN % OF POP. UNDER 15	LITERACY RATE (%) LIFE EXPECTANCY	PER CAPITA GDP HDI
Estonia	17,413 / 1,300,000	69 / 0	Tallinn	Estonian, Ukrainian, Russian, others	Parliamentary democracy; Prime Minister Andrus Ansip	1991 / 15	99/99 / 69/79	$18,500 / 0.883
Finland	130,560 / 5,400,000	65 / 0.2	Helsinki	Finnish, Swedish, Lapp, Russian	Presidential-parliamentary democracy; President Tarja Halonen	1917 / 17	99/99 / 77/83	$34,100 / 0.959
France	212,934 / 63,000,000	77 / 0.4	Paris	French, regional dialects	Presidential-parliamentary democracy; President Nicolas Sarkozy	486 / 18	99/99 / 78/85	$32,600 / 0.961
Germany	137,830 / 81,600,000	73 / -0.2	Berlin	German	Parliamentary democracy; Chancellor Angela Merkel	1871 / 14	99/99 / 77/82	$34,100 / 0.947
Greece	50,950 / 11,300,000	73 / 0.1	Athens	Greek, English, French	Parliamentary democracy; Prime Minister Georgios Papandreou	1829 / 14	98/94 / 77/82	$31,000 / 0.942
Hungary	35,919 / 10,000,000	67 / -0.3	Budapest	Hungarian, others	Parliamentary democracy; Prime Minister Viktor Orbán	1001 / 15	99/99 / 70/78	$18,800 / 0.879
Iceland	39,768 / 300,000	93 / 0.9	Reykjavík	Icelandic	Parliamentary democracy; Prime Minister Jóhanna Sigurdardóttir	1944 / 21	99/99 / 80/83	$39,600 / 0.969
Ireland	27,135 / 4,500,000	60 / 1.0	Dublin	English, Gaelic	Parliamentary democracy; Prime Minister Brian Cowen	1921 / 21	99/99 / 77/82	$41,000 / 0.965
Italy	116,320 / 60,500,000	68 / 0	Rome	Italian, German, French, Slovene	Parliamentary democracy; Prime Minister Silvio Berlusconi	1861 / 14	99/98 / 79/84	$29,900 / 0.951
Kosovo[3]	4,203 / 2,300,000	NA / 1.4	Pristina	Albanian, Serbian, others	Presidential-parliamentary democracy (transitional); Prime Minister Hashim Thaçi	2008 / 31	97/88 / 67/71	$2,500 / NA
Latvia	24,942 / 2,200,000	68 / -0.4	Riga	Lettish, Lithuanian, Russian, others	Parliamentary democracy; Prime Minister Valdis Dombrovskis	1991 / 14	99/99 / 67/78	$14,400 / 0.866
Liechtenstein	62 / 40,000	15 / 0.4	Vaduz	German, Alemannic dialect	Constitutional monarchy; Prince Alois	1719 / 16	99/99 / 79/82	$122,100 / 0.951
Lithuania	25,174 / 3,300,000	67 / -0.1	Vilnius	Lithuanian, Polish, Russian	Presidential-parliamentary democracy; President Dalia Grybauskaite	1991 / 15	99/99 / 66/78	$15,500 / 0.870
Luxembourg	999 / 500,000	83 / 0.4	Luxembourg	Luxembourgish, German, French, English	Parliamentary democracy; Prime Minister Jean-Claude Juncker	1839 / 18	99/99 / 78/83	$79,600 / 0.960
Macedonia	9,927 / 2,100,000	65 / 0.2	Skopje	Macedonian, Albanian, others	Presidential-parliamentary democracy; Prime Minister Nikola Gruevski	1991 / 19	98/94 / 71/76	$9,100 / 0.817
Malta	124 / 400,000	94 / 0.2	Valletta	Maltese, English	Parliamentary democracy; Prime Minister Lawrence Gonzi	1964 / 16	92/94 / 77/82	$24,300 / 0.902
Moldova	13,012 / 4,100,000	41 / 0	Chisinau	Moldovan, Russian, Gagauz	Parliamentary democracy; Acting President Mihai Ghimpu[4]	1991 / 17	99/99 / 66/73	$2,300 / 0.720
Monaco	1 / 40,000	100 / 0	Monaco	French, English, Italian, Monegasque	Constitutional monarchy; Prince Albert II	1419 / 13	99/99 / NA	$30,000 / NA
Montenegro	5,333 / 600,000	64 / 0.4	Podgorica	Montenegrin, Serbian, Bosniak, Albanian	Presidential-parliamentary democracy; President Filip Vujanovic	2006 / 20	NA / 71/76	$9,800 / 0.834
Netherlands	15,768 / 16,600,000	66 / 0.3	Amsterdam	Dutch	Parliamentary democracy; Prime Minister Jan Peter Balkenende	1579 / 18	99/99 / 78/82	$39,500 / 0.964
Norway	125,050 / 4,900,000	80 / 0.4	Oslo	Norwegian, Lapp, Finnish	Parliamentary democracy; Prime Minister Jens Stoltenberg	1905 / 19	99/99 / 79/83	$57,400 / 0.971
Poland	124,807 / 38,200,000	61 / 0.1	Warsaw	Polish	Presidential-parliamentary democracy; President Bronislaw Komorowski	1918 / 15	99/99 / 71/80	$17,900 / 0.880
Portugal	35,514 / 10,700,000	55 / -0.1	Lisbon	Portuguese	Presidential-parliamentary democracy; Prime Minister José Sócrates	1140 / 15	96/91 / 75/82	$21,700 / 0.909

[3] Kosovo declared its independence from Serbia on February 17, 2008. As of September 2010, it is recognized by only 70 countries.
[4] Postponed September 2010 elections by Parliament not rescheduled at press time.

119

EUROPE

COUNTRY	AREA (SQ MI) POPULATION	URBAN POP. % POP. RISE %/YEAR	CAPITAL	LANGUAGES	POLITICAL SYSTEM & HEAD OF GOVERNMENT	DATE OF ORIGIN % OF POP. UNDER 15	LITERACY RATE (%) LIFE EXPECTANCY	PER CAPITA GDP HDI
Romania	92,042	55	Bucharest	Romanian, Hungarian, German	Presidential-parliamentary democracy; President Traian Basescu	1878	98/96	$11,500
	21,500,000	−0.2				15	69/76	0.837
Russia	6,592,819	73	Moscow	Russian, others	Dominant party; President Dmitry Medvedev	1991	99/99	$15,100
	141,900,000	−0.2				15	62/74	0.817
San Marino	23	84	San Marino	Italian	Parliamentary democracy; Co-Captains Regent elected every six months from the Great and General Council	301	97/95	$41,900
	30,000	0.3				15	80/86	NA
Serbia	34,115	58	Belgrade	Serbo-Croatian, Albanian	Presidential-parliamentary democracy (transitional); President Boris Tadic	1992	99/94	$10,600
	7,300,000	−0.5				15	71/76	0.826
Slovakia	18,923	55	Bratislava	Slovak, Hungarian	Parliamentary democracy; Prime Minister Iveta Radicová	1993	99/99	$21,100
	5,400,000	0.2				15	71/79	0.880
Slovenia	7,819	50	Ljubljana	Slovenian, Serbo-Croatian, others	Parliamentary democracy; Prime Minister Borut Pahor	1991	99/99	$27,700
	2,100,000	0.2				14	76/82	0.929
Spain	195,363	77	Madrid	Castilian Spanish, Catalan, Galician, Basque	Parliamentary democracy; Prime Minister José Luis Rodríguez Zapatero	1492	99/97	$33,600
	47,100,000	0.3				15	78/84	0.955
Sweden	173,730	84	Stockholm	Swedish, Lapp, Finnish	Parliamentary democracy; Prime Minister Fredrik Reinfeldt	1523	99/99	$36,600
	9,400,000	0.2				17	79/83	0.963
Switzerland	15,942	73	Bern	German, French, Italian, Romansch, others	Parliamentary democracy; rotating President from seven-member Federal Council	1291	99/99	$41,400
	7,800,000	0.2				15	80/84	0.960
Ukraine	233,089	69	Kiev	Ukrainian, Russian, Romanian, Polish, Hungarian	Presidential-parliamentary democracy; President Viktor Yanukovych	1991	99/99	$6,300
	45,900,000	−0.4				14	63/74	0.796
United Kingdom (England, Scotland, Wales, N. Ireland)	94,548	80	London	English, Welsh, Scottish, Gaelic	Parliamentary democracy; Prime Minister David Cameron	circa 900	99/99	$34,800
	62,200,000	0.4				18	77/82	0.947
Vatican City	109 acres	100	Vatican City	Italian, Latin, others	Papal state; Pope Benedict XVI	1929	100	NA
	826	0				NA	NA	NA

ASIA

COUNTRY	AREA (SQ MI) POPULATION	URBAN POP. % POP. RISE %/YEAR	CAPITAL	LANGUAGES	POLITICAL SYSTEM & HEAD OF GOVERNMENT	DATE OF ORIGIN % OF POP. UNDER 15	LITERACY RATE (%) LIFE EXPECTANCY	PER CAPITA GDP HDI
Afghanistan	251,772	22	Kabul	Pashtu, Afghan Persian, Turkic, others	Transitional democracy, territory disputed by factions; President Hamid Karzai	1919	43/13	$1,000
	29,100,000	2.1				44	44/44	0.352
Armenia	11,506	64	Yerevan	Armenian, Russian, others	Presidential-parliamentary democracy (transitional); President Serzh Sarkisyan	1991	99/99	$5,500
	3,100,000	0.6				20	68/75	0.798
Azerbaijan	33,436	54	Baku	Azeri, Russian, Armenian, others	Dominant party; President Ilham Aliyev	1991	99/98	$10,400
	9,000,000	1.1				23	70/75	0.788
Bahrain	266	100	Manama	Arabic, English, Farsi, Urdu	Monarchy; King Hamad bin Isa al-Khalifah	1971	89/84	$38,800
	1,300,000	1.3				20	73/77	0.895
Bangladesh	55,598	25	Dhaka	Bengali, English	Presidential-parliamentary (transitional); Prime Minister Sheikh Hasina Wajed	1971	54/41	$1,500
	164,400,000	1.5				32	65/67	0.543
Bhutan	18,147	32	Thimphu	Dzongkha, Tibetan and Nepalese dialects	Parliamentary democracy in transition from monarchy; Prime Minister Jigmi Thinley	1949	60/34	$4,700
	700,000	1.7				31	67/68	0.619
Brunei	2,228	72	Bandar Seri Begawan	Malay, English, Chinese	Monarchy; Sultan Hassanal Bolkiah	1984	95/90	$51,200
	400,000	1.3				27	75/80	0.920
Cambodia	69,900	20	Phnom Penh	Khmer, French	Dominant party; Prime Minister Hun Sen	1949	85/64	$1,900
	15,100,000	1.6				35	59/63	0.593
China	3,696,100	47	Beijing	Mandarin, other Chinese languages, other languages	One-party dictatorship; President Hu Jintao	1912	96/88	$6,600
	1,338,100,000	0.5				18	72/76	0.772
Cyprus[5]	3,571	62	Nicosia	Greek, Turkish, English	Presidential-parliamentary democracy; President Dimitris Christofias	1960	99/96	$21,000
	1,100,000	0.6				18	77/80	0.914

5 Does not include separate Turkish Cypriot-controlled area in north.

ASIA

COUNTRY	AREA (SQ MI) POPULATION	URBAN POP. % POP. RISE %/YEAR	CAPITAL	LANGUAGES	POLITICAL SYSTEM & HEAD OF GOVERNMENT	DATE OF ORIGIN % OF POP. UNDER 15	LITERACY RATE (%) LIFE EXPECTANCY	PER CAPITA GDP HDI
Georgia	26,911	53	Tbilisi	Georgian, Russian, Armenian, Azeri, Ossetian, others	Presidential-parliamentary democracy; President Mikheil Saakashvili	1991	99/99	$4,400
	4,600,000	0.3				17	69/79	0.778
India	1,269,340	29	New Delhi	Hindi, English, Bengali, many others	Parliamentary democracy; Prime Minister Manmohan Singh	1947	73/48	$3,100
	1,188,800,000	1.5				32	63/65	0.612
Indonesia	735,355	43	Jakarta	Bahasa Indonesian, English, Dutch, others	Parliamentary democracy; President Susilo Bambang Yudhoyono	1945	94/87	$4,000
	235,500,000	1.4				28	69/73	0.734
Iran	630,575	69	Tehran	Farsi, Turkic, Kurdish, Luri, others	Presidential-parliamentary under religious control; President Mahmoud Ahmadinejad	1502	84/70	$12,500
	75,100,000	1.3				28	70/73	0.782
Iraq	169,236	67	Baghdad	Arabic, Kurdish, Assyrian, Armenian	Transitional to parliamentary democracy; Prime Minister Nuri al-Maliki	1932	84/64	$3,800
	31,500,000	2.6				41	64/72	NA
Israel[6]	8,131	92	Jerusalem	Hebrew, Arabic, English	Parliamentary democracy; Prime Minister Benjamin Netanyahu	1948	99/96	$28,400
	7,600,000	1.6				28	79/83	0.935
Japan	145,869	86	Tokyo	Japanese	Parliamentary democracy; Prime Minister Naoto Kan	660 B.C.	99/99	$32,700
	127,400,000	0				13	79/86	0.960
Jordan	34,444	83	Amman	Arabic, English	Constitutional monarchy; King Abdullah II	1946	95/85	$5,200
	6,500,000	2.6				37	72/74	0.770
Kazakhstan	1,049,151	54	Astana	Kazakh, Russian, Ukrainian, others	Dominant party; President Nursultan Nazarbayev	1991	99/99	$11,800
	16,300,000	1.4				24	63/74	0.804
Korea, North	46,541	60	Pyongyang	Korean	Communist dictatorship; General Secretary Kim Jong Il	1945	99/99	$1,900
	22,800,000	0.5				22	61/66	NA
Korea, South	38,324	82	Seoul	Korean, English	Presidential-parliamentary democracy; President Lee Myung Bak	1945	99/97	$28,100
	48,900,000	0.4				17	77/83	0.937
Kuwait	6,880	98	Kuwait	Arabic, English	Monarchy; Emir Sabah al-Ahmad al-Jabir al-Sabah	1961	94/91	$52,800
	3,100,000	2.0				23	76/80	0.916
Kyrgyzstan	76,641	35	Bishkek	Kirghiz, Russian	Presidential-parliamentary (transitional after coup); Interim President Roza Otunbayeva	1991	99/98	$2,200
	5,300,000	1.6				29	64/72	0.710
Laos	91,429	27	Vientiane	Lao, French, English, others	Communist one-party state; President Choummaly Sayasone	1949	83/63	$2,100
	6,400,000	2.1				39	63/66	0.619
Lebanon	4,015	87	Beirut	Arabic, French, Armenian, English	Presidential-parliamentary democracy; President Michel Suleiman	1943	93/82	$13,200
	4,300,000	1.5				25	70/74	0.803
Malaysia	127,317	63	Kuala Lumpur	Malay, English, Chinese languages, many others	Dominant party; Prime Minister Najib Tun Razak	1957	92/85	$14,900
	28,900,000	1.6				32	72/77	0.829
Maldives	116	35	Malé	Maldivian Divehi, English	Presidential-parliamentary democracy (transitional); President Mohamed Nasheed	1965	96/96	$4,300
	300,000	1.9				30	72/74	0.771
Mongolia	604,826	60	Ulaanbaatar	Khalkha Mongolian, Turkic, Russian, Chinese	Presidential-parliamentary democracy; Prime Minister Sükhbaataryn Batbold	1921	98/98	$3,100
	2,800,000	1.9				33	63/70	0.727
Myanmar (Burma)	261,228	31	Naypyidaw Myodaw	Burmese, others	Military rule; General Than Shwe	1948	94/86	$1,100
	53,400,000	0.9				27	56/60	0.586
Nepal	56,826	17	Kathmandu	Nepali, others	Parliamentary democracy (transitional from monarchy); Prime Minister Jhalanath Khanal	1768	63/35	$1,200
	28,000,000	1.9				37	64/65	0.553
Oman	82,031	72	Muscat	Arabic, English, Baluchi, Urdu, others	Monarchy; Sultan Qaboos bin Said al-Said	1650	87/74	$25,000
	3,100,000	1.8				29	70/74	0.846
Pakistan	307,375	35	Islamabad	Urdu, Punjabi, Sindhi, Siraiki, English, others	Presidential-parliamentary (transitional from military); President Asif Ali Zardari	1947	63/36	$2,500
	184,800,000	2.3				38	66/67	0.572
Philippines	115,830	63	Manila	Filipino, English	Presidential-legislative democracy; President Benigno Aquino III	1898	93/93	$3,300
	94,000,000	2.1				33	70/74	0.751

[6] Does not include Israeli-occupied parts of the West Bank.

121

ASIA

COUNTRY	AREA (SQ MI) / POPULATION	URBAN POP. % / POP. RISE %/YEAR	CAPITAL	LANGUAGES	POLITICAL SYSTEM & HEAD OF GOVERNMENT	DATE OF ORIGIN / % OF POP. UNDER 15	LITERACY RATE (%) / LIFE EXPECTANCY	PER CAPITA GDP / HDI
Qatar	4,247	100	Doha	Arabic, English	Monarchy; Emir Hamad bin Khalifa al-Thani	1971	89/89	$119,500
	1,700,000	0.8				15	75/77	0.910
Saudi Arabia	829,996	81	Riyadh	Arabic	Monarchy; King Abdallah bin Abd al-Aziz Al Saud	1932	85/71	$20,600
	29,200,000	2.6				38	74/78	0.843
Singapore	239	100	Singapore	Chinese, Malay, Tamil, English	Dominant party; Prime Minister Lee Hsien Loong	1965	97/89	$52,200
	5,100,000	0.6				18	79/84	0.944
Sri Lanka	25,332	15	Colombo	Tamil, Sinhala, English	Presidential-parliamentary democracy; President Mahinda Rajapakse	1948	92/89	$4,500
	20,700,000	1.2				26	72/76	0.759
Syria	71,498	54	Damascus	Arabic, Kurdish, Armenian, French, others	Dominant party; President Bashar al-Assad	1946	86/74	$4,600
	22,500,000	2.5				36	72/76	0.742
Taiwan	13,969	78	Taipei	Mandarin Chinese, Taiwanese, others	Presidential-parliamentary democracy; President Ma Ying-jeou	1949	96	$32,000
	23,200,000	0.2				16	75/82	NA
Tajikistan	55,251	26	Dushanbe	Tajik, Russian	Dominant party; President Emomalii Rakhmon	1991	99/99	$1,900
	7,600,000	2.4				38	64/69	0.688
Thailand	198,116	31	Bangkok	Thai, English, regional dialects	Transitional after military coup; Prime Minister Abhisit Vejjajiva	1238	95/91	$8,200
	68,100,000	0.6				22	66/72	0.783
Timor-Leste (East Timor)	5,741	22	Dili	Tetun, Portuguese, Indonesian, English	Presidential-parliamentary democracy (transitional); Prime Minister Xanana Gusmão	2002	59	$2,400
	1,200,000	3.1				45	60/62	0.489
Turkey	299,158	76	Ankara	Turkish, Kurdish, Arabic	Parliamentary democracy; Prime Minister Recep Tayyip Erdogan	1923	95/80	$11,400
	73,600,000	1.2				26	69/74	0.806
Turkmenistan	188,456	47	Ashgabat	Turkmen, Uzbek, Russian, others	Presidential dictatorship; President Gurbanguly Berdymukhammedov	1991	99/98	$6,700
	5,200,000	1.4				31	61/69	0.739
United Arab Emirates	32,278	83	Abu Dhabi	Arabic, Farsi, English, Hindi, Urdu	Federation of traditional monarchies; President Khalifa bin Zayid al-Nuhayyan	1971	76/82	$38,900
	5,400,000	1.4				19	77/79	0.903
Uzbekistan	172,741	36	Tashkent	Uzbek, Russian, Tajik, others	Presidential dictatorship; President Islam Karimov	1991	99/99	$2,800
	28,100,000	1.8				33	65/71	0.710
Vietnam	128,066	28	Hanoi	Vietnamese, French, Chinese, English, Khmer, others	Communist one-party state; Prime Minister Nguyen Tan Dung	1945	94/87	$2,900
	88,900,000	1.2				25	72/76	0.725
Yemen	203,849	29	Sanaa	Arabic	Dominant party; President Ali Abdullah Saleh	1990	71/30	$2,500
	23,600,000	3.0				45	62/64	0.575

OCEANIA

COUNTRY	AREA (SQ MI) / POPULATION	URBAN POP. % / POP. RISE %/YEAR	CAPITAL	LANGUAGES	POLITICAL SYSTEM & HEAD OF GOVERNMENT	DATE OF ORIGIN / % OF POP. UNDER 15	LITERACY RATE (%) / LIFE EXPECTANCY	PER CAPITA GDP / HDI
Australia	2,988,888	82	Canberra	English, aboriginal languages	Parliamentary democracy; Prime Minister Julia Gillard	1901	99/99	$40,000
	22,400,000	0.7				19	79/84	0.970
Fiji	7,054	51	Suva	English, Fijian, Hindustani	Military; Interim Prime Minister Commodore Voreqe Bainimarama	1970	96/92	$3,900
	900,000	1.7				29	66/71	0.741
Kiribati	282	44	Tarawa	English, Gilbertese	Presidential-legislative democracy; President Anote Tong	1979	NA	$6,100
	100,000	1.8				36	59/63	NA
Marshall Islands	69	68	Majuro	English, Marshallese dialects, Japanese	Parliamentary democracy and traditional chiefs; President Jurelang Zedkaia	1986	94/94	$2,500
	100,000	2.8				41	64/67	NA
Micronesia	270	22	Palikir	English, Trukese, Pohnpein, Yapese, Kosraean	Parliamentary democracy; President Emanuel Mori	1986	91/88	$2,200
	100,000	1.9				37	67/68	NA
Nauru	9	100	Yaren District	Nauruan, English	Parliamentary democracy; Interim President Marcus Stephen (during state of emergency)	1968	NA	$5,000
	10,000	1.9				39	55/57	NA

OCEANIA

COUNTRY	AREA (SQ MI) POPULATION	URBAN POP. % POP. RISE %/YEAR	CAPITAL	LANGUAGES	POLITICAL SYSTEM & HEAD OF GOVERNMENT	DATE OF ORIGIN % OF POP. UNDER 15	LITERACY RATE (%) LIFE EXPECTANCY	PER CAPITA GDP HDI
New Zealand	104,452	86	Wellington	English, Maori	Parliamentary democracy; Prime Minister John Key	1907	99/99	$27,400
	4,400,000	0.8				21	78/82	0.950
Palau	178	78	Melekeok	English, Sonsorolese, Palauan, others	Presidential-legislative democracy and traditional chiefs; President Johnson Toribiong	1994	93/90	$8,100
	20,000	0.6				24	66/72	NA
Papua New Guinea	178,703	13	Port Moresby	English, pidgin English, Motu, many others	Parliamentary democracy; Prime Minister Sir Michael Somare	1975	63/51	$2,300
	6,800,000	2.2				40	57/62	0.541
Samoa	1,097	22	Apia	Samoan, English	Parliamentary democracy and traditional chiefs; Prime Minister Tuilaepa Sailele Malielegaoi	1962	99/99	$5,400
	200,000	2.0				40	72/74	0.771
Solomon Islands	11,158	17	Honiara	Melanesian pidgin, English, others	Parliamentary democracy; Prime Minister Danny Philip	1978	NA	$2,500
	500,000	2.5				41	62/63	0.610
Tonga	290	23	Nuku'alofa	Tongan, English	Monarchy; King George Tupou V	1970	99/99	$6,300
	100,000	2.2				38	67/73	0.768
Tuvalu	10	47	Funafuti	Tuvaluan, English	Parliamentary democracy; Prime Minister Willy Telavi	1978	NA	$1,600
	10,000	1.4				32	62/65	NA
Vanuatu	4,707	24	Port-Vila	English, French, Bislama	Parliamentary democracy; Prime Minister Edward Natapei	1980	74	$5,300
	200,000	2.5				40	66/69	0.693

AFRICA

COUNTRY	AREA (SQ MI) POPULATION	URBAN POP. % POP. RISE %/YEAR	CAPITAL	LANGUAGES	POLITICAL SYSTEM & HEAD OF GOVERNMENT	DATE OF ORIGIN % OF POP. UNDER 15	LITERACY RATE (%) LIFE EXPECTANCY	PER CAPITA GDP HDI
Algeria	919,591	63	Algiers	Arabic, French, Berber dialects	Dominant party; Government in transition	1962	80/60	$7,100
	36,000,000	1.8				28	71/74	0.754
Angola	481,351	57	Luanda	Portuguese, Bantu, others	Presidential-parliamentary (transitional); President José Eduardo dos Santos	1975	83/54	$8,400
	19,000,000	2.5				45	45/49	0.564
Benin	43,483	41	Porto-Novo	French, Fon, Yoruba, others	Presidential-legislative democracy; President Yayi Boni	1960	48/23	$1,500
	9,800,000	3.0				45	57/60	0.492
Botswana	224,606	60	Gaborone	English, Setswana	Parliamentary democracy and traditional chiefs; President Ian Khama	1966	80/82	$12,800
	1,800,000	1.9				33	55/55	0.694
Burkina Faso	105,792	23	Ouagadougou	French, Sudanic languages	Presidential-parliamentary democracy (transitional); President Blaise Compaoré	1960	29/15	$1,200
	16,200,000	3.4				46	51/54	0.389
Burundi	10,745	10	Bujumbura	Kirundi, French, Swahili	Presidential-legislative democracy (transitional); President Pierre Nkurunziza	1962	67/52	$300
	8,500,000	2.1				41	49/52	0.394
Cameroon	183,568	53	Yaoundé	English, French, African languages	Dominant party; President Paul Biya	1960	77/60	$2,300
	20,000,000	2.3				41	50/52	0.523
Cape Verde	1,556	61	Praia	Portuguese, Crioulo	Presidential-parliamentary democracy; Prime Minister José Maria Neves	1975	86/69	$3,600
	500,000	2.0				35	69/76	0.708
Central African Republic	240,533	38	Bangui	French, Sangho, Arabic, Hunsa, Swahili	Presidential-parliamentary democracy (transitional); President François Bozizé	1960	65/34	$700
	4,800,000	2.2				41	47/50	0.369
Chad	495,753	27	N'Djamena	French, Arabic, Sara, others	Dominant party; President Idriss Déby	1960	41/13	$1,900
	11,500,000	2.9				46	47/50	0.392
Comoros	861	28	Moroni	Arabic, French, Comoran	Presidential-parliamentary; President Elect Ikililou Dhoinine	1975	64/49	$1,000
	700,000	2.6				38	62/66	0.576
Congo, Democratic Republic	905,351	33	Kinshasa	French, Lingala, Kingwana, Kikongo, Tshiluba	In transition from military to presidential-parliamentary; President Joseph Kabila	1960	81/54	$300
	67,800,000	2.9				48	46/49	0.389
Congo, Republic	132,046	60	Brazzaville	French, Lingala, Mono-kutuba, Kikongo, others	Military (transitional); President Denis Sassou-Nguesso	1960	90/78	$3,900
	3,900,000	2.5				42	52/54	0.601

123

AFRICA

COUNTRY	AREA (SQ MI) POPULATION	URBAN POP. % POP. RISE %/YEAR	CAPITAL	LANGUAGES	POLITICAL SYSTEM & HEAD OF GOVERNMENT	DATE OF ORIGIN % OF POP. UNDER 15	LITERACY RATE (%) LIFE EXPECTANCY	PER CAPITA GDP HDI
Côte d'Ivoire (Ivory Coast)	124,502	50	Yamoussoukro	French, Dioula, others	Presidential-parliamentary (transitional); President Laurent Gbagbo	1960	61/39	$1,700
	22,000,000	2.4				40	51/54	0.484
Djibouti	8,958	76	Djibouti	French, Arabic, Somali, Afar	President Ismail Omar Guelleh	1977	78/58	$2,700
	900,000	1.8				37	54/57	0.520
Egypt	386,660	43	Cairo	Arabic, English, French	Government in transition	1922	83/59	$6,000
	80,400,000	2.1				33	69/75	0.703
Equatorial Guinea	10,830	39	Malabo	Spanish, French, pidgin English, Fang, Bubi, Ibo	Presidential dictatorship; President Teodoro Obiang Nguema Mbasogo	1968	93/81	$37,500
	700,000	2.3				42	48/51	0.719
Eritrea	45,405	21	Asmara	Amharic, Arabic, Afar, Tigrinya, Tigre, many others	One-party dictatorship; President Isaias Afewerki	1993	70/48	$700
	5,200,000	2.9				42	57/62	0.472
Ethiopia	426,371	16	Addis Ababa	Amharic, Tigrinya, Arabic, Orominga, English, others	Dominant party; Prime Minister Meles Zenawi	1000 B.C.	50/35	$900
	85,000,000	2.7				44	54/57	0.414
Gabon	103,347	84	Libreville	French, Fang, Myene, Bateke, others	Dominant party; President Ali Ondimba Bongo	1965	48/33	$14,000
	1,500,000	1.9				43	54/57	0.456
Gambia	4,363	54	Banjul	English, Mandinka, Wolof, Fula, others	Dominant party; President Yahya Jammeh	1965	48/33	$1,400
	1,800,000	2.7				43	54/57	0.456
Ghana	92,100	48	Accra	English, Akan, others	Presidential-parliamentary democracy; President John Atta Mills	1957	66/50	$1,500
	24,000,000	2.2				39	58/61	0.526
Guinea	94,927	28	Conakry	French, various African languages	Republic; President Alpha Condé	1958	43/18	$1,000
	10,800,000	3.0				43	55/58	0.435
Guinea-Bissau	13,946	30	Bissau	Portuguese, Criolo, others	Presidential-legislative (transitional); President Malam Bacai Sanhá	1973	58/27	$1,100
	1,600,000	2.4				43	45/48	0.396
Kenya	224,081	18	Nairobi	English, Swahili, many others	Presidential-parliamentary democracy; President Mwai Kibaki	1963	91/80	$1,600
	40,000,000	2.7				42	56/57	0.541
Lesotho	11,718	23	Maseru	Sesotho, English, Zulu, Xhosa	Parliamentary and traditional chiefs (transitional); Prime Minister Pakalitha Mosisili	1966	75/95	$1,600
	1,900,000	0.9				34	40/43	0.514
Liberia	43,000	58	Monrovia	English, Niger-Congo languages	Presidential-parliamentary democracy (transitional); President Ellen Johnson-Sirleaf	1847	73/42	$400
	4,100,000	3.3				44	54/57	0.442
Libya	679,359	77	Tripoli	Arabic, Italian, English	Dictatorship; Colonel Muammar al-Qaddafi	1951	92/72	$13,400
	6,500,000	1.9				30	72/77	0.847
Madagascar	226,656	31	Antananarivo	French, Malagasy	Presidential-parliamentary democracy (transitional); President Andry Rajoelina	1960	76/63	$1,000
	20,100,000	2.7				43	59/62	0.543
Malawi	45,745	14	Lilongwe	English, Chichewa, others	Presidential-legislative democracy; President Bingu wa Mutharika	1964	76/50	$800
	15,400,000	2.9				46	48/50	0.493
Mali	478,838	33	Bamako	French, Bambara, many others	Presidential-parliamentary democracy; President Amadou Toumani Touré	1960	54/40	$1,200
	15,200,000	3.1				48	50/53	0.371
Mauritania	395,954	40	Nouakchott	Hasaniya Arabic, Pulaar, Soninke, Wolof, French	Presidential-legislative (transitional); President Mohamed Ould Abdel Aziz	1960	60/43	$2,000
	3,400,000	2.3				40	55/59	0.520
Mauritius	788	42	Port Louis	English, Creole, French, Hindi, Urdu, Hakka, Bojpoori	Parliamentary democracy; Prime Minister Navin Ramgoolam	1968	88/81	$13,000
	1,300,000	0.5				22	69/76	0.804
Morocco	172,413	57	Rabat	Arabic, Berber dialects, French	Constitutional monarchy; King Muhammad VI	1956	66/40	$4,700
	31,900,000	1.5				29	69/73	0.654
Mozambique	309,494	31	Maputo	Portuguese, African languages	Presidential-parliamentary democracy; President Armando Guebuza	1975	64/33	$900
	23,400,000	2.3				44	47/49	0.402
Namibia	318,259	35	Windhoek	Afrikaans, German, English, local African languages	Presidential-parliamentary democracy; President Hifikepunye Pohamba	1990	87/84	$6,600
	2,200,000	1.9				38	60/62	0.686

AFRICA

COUNTRY	AREA (SQ MI) POPULATION	URBAN POP. % POP. RISE %/YEAR	CAPITAL	LANGUAGES	POLITICAL SYSTEM & HEAD OF GOVERNMENT	DATE OF ORIGIN % OF POP. UNDER 15	LITERACY RATE (%) LIFE EXPECTANCY	PER CAPITA GDP HDI
Niger	489,189	20	Niamey	French, Hausa, Djerma	Military (transitional); Chairman Salou Djibo	1960	43/15	$700
	15,900,000	3.5				49	48/49	0.340
Nigeria	356,668	47	Abuja	English, Hausa, Yoruba, Ibo, Fulani	Presidential-legislative democracy; President Goodluck Jonathan	1960	76/61	$2,300
	158,300,000	2.4				43	47/48	0.511
Rwanda	10,170	17	Kigali	Kinyarwanda, French, English, Kiswahili	Dominant party; President Paul Kagame	1962	76/65	$1,000
	10,400,000	2.9				42	50/53	0.460
São Tomé and Príncipe	371	58	São Tomé	Portuguese	Presidential-parliamentary democracy; President Fradique de Menezes	1975	92/78	$1,700
	200,000	2.9				44	64/69	0.651
Senegal	75,954	41	Dakar	French, Wolof, Pulaar, Diola, Mandingo	Presidential-parliamentary democracy; President Abdoulaye Wade	1960	51/29	$1,600
	12,500,000	2.8				44	54/57	0.464
Seychelles	174	53	Victoria	English, French, Creole	Presidential-legislative democracy; President James Michel	1976	91/92	$20,800
	100,000	1.0				22	68/78	0.845
Sierra Leone	27,699	36	Freetown	English, Mende, Temne, Krio	Presidential-legislative democracy; President Ernest Bai Koroma	1961	47/24	$900
	5,800,000	2.4				43	46/49	0.365
Somalia	246,201	34	Mogadishu	Somali, Arabic, Italian, English	Limited government disputed by factions	1960	50/26	$600
	9,400,000	3.0				45	48/51	NA
South Africa	471,444	52	Cape Town, Pretoria, and Bloemfontein	English, Afrikaans, Zulu, Xhosa, Swazi, Sotho, others	Parliamentary democracy; President Jacob Zuma	1910	87/86	$10,300
	49,900,000	0.9				31	54/57	0.683
Sudan	967,494	38	Khartoum	Arabic, Nubian, Ta Bedawie, English, others	Presidential-legislative (military-dominated); President Omar Hassan Ahmad al-Bashir	1956	72/51	$2,300
	43,200,000	2.2				41	57/60	0.531
Swaziland	6,703	22	Mbabane and Lobamba	English, siSwati	Monarchy; King Mswati III	1968	83/81	$4,400
	1,200,000	1.5				40	46/45	0.572
Tanzania	364,900	25	Dar es Salaam	Kiswahili, English, Arabic, many others	Dominant party; President Jakaya Kikwete	1964	78/62	$1,400
	45,000,000	3.0				45	55/56	0.530
Togo	21,927	40	Lomé	French, Ewe, Mina, Dagomba, Kabye	Dominant party; President Faure Gnassingbé	1960	75/47	$900
	6,800,000	2.5				41	60/63	0.499
Tunisia	63,170	66	Tunis	Arabic, French	Dominant party; President Zine El Abidine Ben Ali	1956	83/65	$8,200
	10,500,000	1.2				24	72/76	0.769
Uganda	93,066	13	Kampala	English, Luganda, Swahili, others	Dominant party; President Yoweri Museveni	1962	77/58	$1,200
	33,800,000	3.4				49	52/53	0.514
Zambia	290,583	37	Lusaka	English, Bemba, Tonga, others	Presidential-legislative democracy (transitional); President Rupiah Banda	1964	87/75	$1,600
	13,300,000	2.5				46	41/42	0.481
Zimbabwe	150,873	37	Harare	English, Shona, Sindebele, others	Dominant party; President Robert Mugabe	1980	94/87	$100
	12,600,000	1.3				42	41/44	NA

THE MIDDLE EAST

COUNTRY	AREA (SQ MI) POPULATION	URBAN POP. % POP. RISE %/YEAR	CAPITAL	LANGUAGES	POLITICAL SYSTEM & HEAD OF GOVERNMENT	DATE OF ORIGIN % OF POP. UNDER 15	LITERACY RATE (%) LIFE EXPECTANCY	PER CAPITA GDP HDI
Bahrain	266	100	Manama	Arabic, English, Farsi, Urdu	Monarchy; King Hamad bin Isa al-Khalifah	1971	89/84	$38,800
	1,300,000	1.3				20	73/77	0.895
Cyprus[7]	3,571	62	Nicosia	Greek, Turkish, English	Presidential-parliamentary (divided); Presidents Dimitris Christofias and Dervis Eroglu	1960	99/96	$21,000
	1,100,000	0.6				18	77/80	0.914
Egypt	386,660	43	Cairo	Arabic, English, French	Government in transition	1922	83/59	$6,000
	80,400,000	2.1				33	69/75	0.703
Iran	630,575	69	Tehran	Farsi, Turkic, Kurdish, Luri, others	Presidential-parliamentary under religious control; President Mahmoud Ahmadinejad	1502	84/70	$12,500
	75,100,000	1.3				28	70/73	0.782

[7] Does not include separate Turkish Cypriot-controlled area in the north.

| COUNTRY | AREA (SQ MI) | URBAN POP. % | CAPITAL | LANGUAGES | POLITICAL SYSTEM & HEAD OF GOVERNMENT | DATE OF ORIGIN | LITERACY RATE (%) | PER CAPITA GDP |
	POPULATION	POP. RISE %/YEAR				% OF POP. UNDER 15	LIFE EXPECTANCY	HDI
Iraq	169,236	67	Baghdad	Arabic, Kurdish, Assyrian, Armenian	Transitional to parliamentary democracy; results of March 2010 elections disputed at press time	1932	84/64	$3,800
	31,500,000	2.6				41	64/72	NA
Israel[8]	8,131	92	Jerusalem	Hebrew, Arabic, English	Parliamentary democracy; Prime Minister Benjamin Netanyahu	1948	99/96	$28,400
	7,600,000	1.6				28	79/83	0.935
Jordan	34,444	83	Amman	Arabic, English	Constitutional monarchy; King Abdullah II	1946	95/85	$5,200
	6,500,000	2.6				38	72/74	0.770
Kuwait	6,880	98	Kuwait	Arabic, English	Monarchy; Emir Sheikh Sabah al-Ahmad al-Jabir al-Sabah	1961	94/91	$52,800
	3,100,000	2.0				23	76/80	0.916
Lebanon	4,015	87	Beirut	Arabic, French, Armenian, English	Presidential-parliamentary democracy; President Michel Suleiman	1943	93/82	$13,200
	4,300,000	1.5				25	70/74	0.803
Oman	82,031	72	Muscat	Arabic, English, Baluchi, Urdu, others	Monarchy; Sultan Qaboos bin Said al-Said	1650	87/74	$25,000
	3,100,000	1.8				29	70/74	0.846
Qatar	4,247	100	Doha	Arabic, English	Monarchy; Emir Hamid bin Khalifa al-Thani	1971	89/89	$119,500
	1,700,000	0.8				15	75/77	0.910
Saudi Arabia	829,996	81	Riyadh	Arabic	Monarchy; King Abdallah bin Abd al-Aziz Al Saud	1932	85/71	$20,600
	29,200,000	2.6				38	74/78	0.843
Syria	71,498	54	Damascus	Arabic, Kurdish, Armenian, French, others	Dominant party; President Bashar al-Assad	1946	86/74	$4,600
	22,500,000	2.5				36	72/76	0.742
Turkey	299,158	76	Ankara	Turkish, Kurdish, Arabic	Parliamentary democracy; Prime Minister Recep Tayyip Erdogan	1923	95/80	$11,400
	73,600,000	1.2				26	69/74	0.806
United Arab Emirates	32,278	83	Abu Dhabi	Arabic, Farsi, English, Hindi, Urdu	Federation of traditional monarchies; President Khalifa bin Zayid al-Nuhayyan	1971	76/82	$38,900
	5,400,000	1.4				19	77/79	0.903
Yemen	203,849	29	Sanaa	Arabic	Dominant party; President Ali Abdullah Saleh	1990	71/30	$2,500
	23,600,000	3.0				45	62/64	0.575

[8] Does not include Israeli-occupied parts of the West Bank.

Index